Bulb
Gardening
with
Derek Fell

Bulb
Gardening
with
Derek Fell

Practical Advice and
Personal Favorites
from the Best-Selling Author
and Television Show Host

FRIEDMAN/FAIRFAX
PUBLISHERS

A FRIEDMAN/FAIRFAX BOOK

Library of Congress Cataloging-in-Publication Data

Fell, Derek.
    Bulb gardening with Derek Fell: practical advice and personal favorites from the best-selling author and television show host.
       p.   cm.
    Includes index.
    ISBN 1-56799-395-8
    1. Bulbs.   I. Title.
SB425.F32 1997
635.9'4—dc21   96-39424
                                      CIP

Editors: Nancy Engel, Susan Lauzau, Celeste Sollod
Art Director: Jeff Batzli
Designer: Susan E. Livingston
Photography Director: Christopher C. Bain
Production Manager: Camille Lee

Color separations by Bright Arts Graphics (Singapore) Pte Ltd.
Printed in the United Kingdom by Butler & Tanner, Ltd.

10   9   8   7   6   5   4   3   2   1

For bulk purchases and special sales, please contact:
Friedman/Fairfax Publishers
Attention: Sales Department
15 West 26th Street
New York, NY 10010
212/685-6610   FAX 212/685-1307

Visit our website:
http://www.metrobooks.com

Frontispiece: Veldheer tulip garden, Holland, Michigan

Dedication

For my three children, Christina, Victoria, and Derek Jr.,

all of whom love gardening

Acknowledgments

In recent years I have greatly enjoyed creating a series of twenty-two theme gardens at my home, Cedaridge Farm, in Bucks County, Pennsylvania, including extensive bulb plantings, starting with the mass flowering of thousands of daffodils in early spring, and concluding with riotous displays of dahlias and gladiolus until heavy frost. Fortunately, my wife, Carolyn, is a professional flower arranger and enjoys helping with the planting.

The success of our bulb plantings, however, would not be possible without the help of my grounds supervisor, Wendy Fields, who ensures that the flower beds are always picture perfect.

Thanks also to Kathy Nelson, my office manager, who helps to keep my extensive photo library organized. Through her dedication and attention to detail, we maintain accurate records of everything that grows at Cedaridge Farm.

Finally, a word of appreciation to Terry Schultz, owner of Lenteboden Bulb Garden in New Hope, Pennsylvania, for allowing me the freedom of his magnificent spring bulb garden for photography. I'd also like to thank Brent and Becky Heath, for the same courtesy at Daffodil Mart, their bulb farm in Gloucester, Virginia; Brecks Bulbs and Dutch Gardens were important sources as well.

Contents

Opposite: A display of tulips and pansies adds color to a path.

Lenteboden bulb garden, Pennsylvania, displays varieties of tulips and daffodils that are evaluated in the spring.

Introduction

When I moved to Cedaridge Farm, my home in Bucks County, Pennsylvania, it had no gardens to speak of—just a solid stone farmhouse and some colonial-style outbuildings surrounded by lawn and mature sugar maple trees. In five years the property blossomed into twenty-two distinct theme areas—such as a vegetable garden, stream garden, and cottage garden—but my very first gardening endeavor here was to plant several thousand daffodils. Like diamonds, daffodils are forever. You plant them once and they come back faithfully every year with little care. I planted the daffodils in autumn as dormant bulbs. Six months later they were in full flower, heralding spring even before my pansies and forget-me-nots could bloom.

It's that way with all bulbs. Some summer-flowering bulbs bloom even faster. Dahlia tubers will flower within three months of planting, as do tuberous begonias, gladiolus, and garden lilies.

My enthusiasm for bulbs first took hold in the Lake District of England, near where William Wordsworth wrote his famous poem about daffodils, "I Wandered Lonely as a Cloud," with its celebratory lines: "Ten thousand saw I at a glance, / Tossing their heads in spritely dance." I fondly recall helping an uncle who lived in the district round up some sheep from a meadow that glistened with thousands of daffodils, a clear-running stream splashing its way among them. I have re-created that memory at Cedaridge Farm so that every spring I am reminded of those happy days exploring the British Lake District.

Since then I have traveled around the world to areas famous for gardens and flowering bulbs. I have marveled at the sea of tulips flowering in the fields and gardens of Holland, with only a ridge of sand dunes separating the brilliantly colored flower fields from the cold Atlantic Ocean. I have stood spellbound in the heart of Namaqualand, the semidesert of South Africa, transfixed at the sight of hundreds of thousands of acres glittering with tender flowering bulbs, such as orange sparaxis, yellow bulbicodiums, and white hooded calla lilies. On the road to Marrakesh, Morocco, I was amazed by the sight of wayside grasslands thick with wild purple gladiolus. In New Zealand I photographed acres of blue and white agapanthus naturalized among sand dunes, their hues echoing the color of pounding surf from the Tasman Sea. And in the mysterious Organ Mountains of Brazil, I saw a colony of perhaps the world's rarest bulb—the *blue amaryllis* (*Worsleya rayneri*)—growing wild among rocky outcrops.

Along the way, several bulb growers have taught me about the growing, selection, and care of bulbs. First and foremost was the late Jan de Graaff, the American lily hybridizer. De Graaff employed me to help introduce his spectacular hybrid garden lilies to Europe.

Then there was the late Charles H. Mueller, a bulb specialist who was my neighbor for many years. He allowed me to photograph his unique and colorful bulb garden near New Hope, Pennsylvania, and each spring he took me to some of the large estate gardens he had planted. Charles established a business selling bulbs by mail, largely through having people visit his garden in the spring. He planted what he called "a living bulb catalog." People could tour the plantings, decide on the varieties and colors they liked, and hand Mueller an order at the end of the tour. The business is still carried on by his friend, Terry Schultz; many of the photographs in this book were taken at Mueller's garden after Terry assumed responsibility for the business.

Calla lilies grow on the slopes of Table Mountain, South Africa, home of many tender bulbs.

Keukenhof bulb garden, in Holland, is one of the world's most visited public gardens, with dozens of theme areas in a woodland setting.

I have also been greatly influenced by the enthusiasm and skills of a remarkable husband-and-wife team, Brent and Becky Heath. They are the brains behind The Daffodil Mart, a business originally established by Brent's grandfather, in Gloucester, Virginia. Many of the bulbs at Colonial Williamsburg were in fact planted by the Heaths.

The culmination of my increasing interest in bulbs was a journey to the fabulous Keukenhof bulb garden, near Amsterdam, in Holland. More than a million people visit this large woodland garden each year to marvel at the displays of daffodils, tulips, and other spring bulbs. I urge every gardener to make the trip. While you are visiting Keukenhof, take a side trip to the Bulbus Hortorum Garden, a living bulb museum where you can see the most important bulb developments dating back to the sixteenth century, when tulips were first introduced to Europe from the gardens of the sultan of Turkey.

But bulbs have been around for much longer than the past few centuries. Edible onion bulbs were cultivated for food even before recorded history. And there is evidence that Egyptians, Greeks, and Romans all cultivated species of daffodils, gladiolus, hyacinths, and crocuses for ornamental value.

More recently, the introduction of the tulip to Europe dates to 1554 when Carolus Clusius, head gardener for the emperor of Austria, received a shipment of bulbs from Sultan Süleyman the Magnificent of Turkey. When Clusius left Austria to work in Holland, he took tulip bulbs with him. The bulbs became such a curiosity that tremendous financial speculation surrounded the development and introduction of new varieties, leading to an era known as "tulipomania." When public interest began to wane, the market collapsed suddenly.

However, enough interest in the tulip remained to prompt some companies to continue their breeding and development work. Today Holland is the chief growing area for most cultivated varieties of tulips seen in home gardens. Even those varieties of bulbs that are not suitable for growing outdoors in Holland's cool climate, like amaryllis, are grown in other areas of the world under the direction of growers from Holland.

In recent years, there has been great concern over the commercial exploitation of bulbs harvested from the wild. For example, Turkey and Pakistan have long exported wild varieties of snow-drops, aconites, cyclamen, species tulips, and other bulbs, depleting huge indigenous colonies and threatening them with extinction. To address this concern, reputable bulb packagers and bulb catalogs now state that none of their bulbs have been harvested from the wild, but were obtained from commercial farms.

Bulb producers have discovered new areas of the world for growing quality bulbs. In North America, the Pacific Northwest is ideal for the production of

Colorful hyacinths are planted informally beside a pond at Cedaridge Farm.

dahlias, lilies, and tulips. The sandy, frost-free hills around Gardena, north of San Diego, California, are perfect for the production of more tender varieties of bulbs, such as ranunculus, freesias, Dutch irises, and gladiolus.

In my own garden I no longer need to concern myself with buying aconites, bluebells, daffodils, Asiatic lilies, and Japanese tiger lilies since they have all happily "naturalized," or propagated themselves. I can simply dig up crowded clumps and spread them around. In fact, naturalizing (also called perennializing) is probably the most satisfying way to grow most bulbs. For special tips on naturalizing, see page 47.

The focus of this book is using flowering bulbs as prominent ornamental plants in the garden. I will discuss how to care for them so they come back every year. I will also give some pointers on growing the hardy varieties if you live in a climate with severe winters, and on growing the more tender varieties if you live in a mild climate. There are also solid ideas for using bulbs creatively in home gardens, illustrated by photographs of actual garden settings, particularly my own garden.

Derek Fell
Cedaridge Farm
Gardenville, Pennsylvania

Planning
and
Planting

Opposite: Daffodil "Flower Record" blooms in a formal garden.

Definition of a Bulb

The term bulb can be applied to "true" bulb-bearing plants such as tulips and daffodils, and to other plants that develop bulbous underground storage organs, including crocus corms, dahlia tubers, and iris rhizomes. The differences between these five terms are largely for botanists.

True bulbs (such as tulips) are usually shaped like onions, and, like onions, made up of fleshy layers with a papery tunic on the outside. They have a rounded base and pointed tip showing which end is up. The mature bulbs produce bulblets around the base, which can be removed to produce new plants identical to the parent.

Corms (such as gladiolus) are solid, mostly flattened and circular in shape. Corms produce cormlets around the base. A premature pointed shoot often emerges from the top of the cormlet.

Tubers (such as begonias) are highly variable in appearance. They are composed of underground stems and are usually lumpy or irregular in shape. It is sometimes difficult to tell which end is up, but even if tubers are planted upside-down, new shoots will still emerge from the top or sides.

Tuberous roots (such as dahlias) are swollen cigar-shaped root sections, which are sometimes held in clusters with a crown of immature shoots on top.

Finally, rhizomes (such as irises) are swollen horizontal underground stems. They are generally oval in shape, with conspicuous roots growing on the bottom, and shoots emerging from the top. For the sake of simplicity it is perfectly acceptable to refer to all of them as bulbs.

Gently squeeze tulip bulbs that are ready for planting to ascertain firmness before planting them pointed end up.

Which End Is Up?

Usually the pointed end of a bulb signifies the part that should be planted "up," but some bulbs (like anemones) have irregular shapes and it can very be difficult to determine which end is the top. With bulbs that have no point and are oddly shaped, you may be able to detect some dried roots, which indicate the bottom of the bulb. But even if you can't figure out which end is up, don't worry. If you plant a bulb upside-down, the growing tip will simply sprout sideways and then reach up toward the soil surface. In other words, the bulb naturally corrects your mistakes.

Caring for Bulbs

After producing leaves and flowers, bulbs store food in their underground organs to help them survive anticipated periods of stress (usually hot, dry summers, cold, freezing winters, or both). They rest in the soil in a dormant condition. When a combination of factors such as moisture and temperature are ideal, the bulbs will break dormancy, produce new green growth, flower, and set seed before dying down and returning to dormancy.

To replenish themselves, bulbs need to keep their leaves after they flower. A cardinal rule of growing bulbs is *never* to cut the leaves, but allow them to die down naturally. It is also vital that the leaves receive adequate light, which enables them to store sufficient food for reblooming. There is a misconception that daffodils and tulips tolerate shade. Though they will bloom the first season in shade, it is likely that these bulbs will dwindle and fail to bloom completely in subsequent years unless the location is only lightly shaded. For more on growing bulbs in the shade, see page 20.

Tying up Bulb Foliage

After bulbs flower, the leaves should be left to die down naturally. With daffodils, this is a particular problem because the leaves will persist for 10 weeks or more, sprawling across the ground. What is the correct way to manage daffodil leaves when the flowers fade and you are left with withering foliage? In public parks you often see the leaves gathered, bent double, and secured with a rubber band or string to keep them looking tidy. This is not recommended. To do their job of replenishing the bulb, daffodil leaves need air circulation around them. Still, if you must do it for the sake of appearances, tying the leaves, as in the picture below, is better than cutting them off at ground level. To avoid the untidy look of beds full of dying foliage, consider relegating daffodils to the edges of your property, against a fence or hedge where later-flowering perennials, like hostas and peonies, will grow up and hide them. Also consider alternating clumps of summer-flowering daylilies with clumps of daffodils. The daylily foliage will hide the spent daffodil foliage quite well.

Staking Bulbs

Dahlias, garden lilies, and gladiolus are examples of summer-flowering bulbs that generally need staking. The traditional way to stake plants is to push a strong bamboo stake into the soil beside the bulb, making sure it is clear of the roots. Then secure the upright stem to the stake with a twist-tie. However, if you have a lot of plants in a bed, this can be tedious. An easier way to support a large expanse of bulbs is to stretch wide wire mesh over the plants when they are young. The plants will push their shoots through the wire and become self-supporting.

Many hardy bulbs require a certain number of days at freezing temperatures, or "cold treatment," before they can rebloom. This is why many tulips and daffodils do not do well in very warm climates unless they have been "preconditioned" (stored for a specific period at cold temperatures).

It generally pays to remove faded flowers so the plants do not set seed. This process, known as deadheading, allows all of the plant's energy to be directed into creating a bigger bulb. In all cases, the bigger the bulb, the better the bloom. At Cedaridge Farm, even with thousands of daffodils naturalized at the edges of the lawn, my wife and I try to deadhead every blossom each season.

With only a few exceptions (calla lilies and elephant ears, for example), bulbs prefer soil that has excellent drainage. Some bulbs, like foxtail lilies, are so fussy about drainage that it may be necessary to make a gravel pit to keep them flourishing from year to year. For more on drainage, see page 19.

It is a mistake to believe that all bulbs will come back year after year with no care. On the contrary, many of them are susceptible to suffocation from weeds and many are heavy feeders. Some bulbs need feeding twice a year to prevent their dwindling and petering out completely.

All things considered, however, bulbs are a lot less trouble to plant and care for than annuals or hardy perennials. Some, like miniature daffodils, are especially good for growing in containers, and many bulbs, like cyclamen and amaryllis, make excellent house plants.

Buying Bulbs

There are two reliable sources for quality bulbs: garden centers and mail-order suppliers. Many popular varieties of spring-flowering bulbs, such as tulips, daffodils, and hyacinths, are widely available in autumn for immediate planting. Most garden centers run clearance sales on whatever they have left a few weeks before they close for the season. Then, when they reopen in spring, they will offer a selection of summer-flowering bulbs to be planted in the spring.

A wider selection of bulb varieties is available from mail-order specialists. Typically they send a preseason catalog in the spring for autumn delivery of autumn-planted bulbs, and another mailing in late summer for bulbs to be planted immediately. The preseason prices are usually discounted to encourage early purchase. Some suppliers send another catalog of summer-flowering bulbs just after Christmas.

Many growers specialize in plant groups, such as garden lilies, irises, and antique bulbs. Several such nurseries are listed on pages 116–117. When you are looking for the rare and unusual, or if you want to build a collection of a particular plant group, these specialty nurseries are the best source.

There are certainly plenty of choices of where to buy bulbs, but how can you be sure of the quality? A bulb is said to be "blind" if it fails to bloom the first season after planting. Blind bulbs can occur when the bulb is too small. Dutch suppliers are pro-

hibited from shipping substandard bulbs into the United States, thus bulbs labeled as "Holland Bulbs" are always reliable. But some companies grow substandard sizes in North America. Be cautious of companies that offer 100 bulbs for $5.00! More than likely, these bulbs will not bloom the first season. It always pays to buy bulbs that are classified as "jumbo" (the best) or "top size" (the next-best grade).

Some of the best bulbs come from production fields of tulips like this one, blooming in early May along the coast of Holland.

To determine if a bulb is diseased, squeeze it. If it feels soft or mushy, it is probably infected with fungus rot or tiny pests such as thrips. Discard and burn these bulbs or return them to the supplier and demand a refund. Bulbs can also turn blind in the soil after planting, usually from rodents eating them or as a result of rot from poor drainage.

Crown imperials partnered with daffodils and tulips flourish in a shady rock garden with well-drained soil.

Drainage

Though a few bulb varieties will tolerate wet feet (notably calla lilies and flag irises), the majority prefer excellent drainage. The most important planting condition for bulbs is soil that does not puddle, and which will drain away excess moisture. To determine if your site drains well, dig a 2-foot (60cm)-deep hole the width of a spade on a dry, sunny day and fill it to the brim with water. Then time how long it takes to drain. If the hole is still full of water after an hour, your site has poor drainage.

The easiest way to improve the site is to create an elevated bed using landscape ties, stones, or bricks. If the site is swampy or boggy and even a raised bed stays moisture-laden, then you may need to dig trenches and lay drainage pipes to take away excess moisture.

Light Requirements

Bulbs generally prefer to be planted in a sunny position, though a few (like cyclamen and caladiums) will tolerate light shade. To test whether you have enough sunlight, stake out your planting area with string and time how long the sun shines on it. A minimum of six hours of sunlight is best. If shade from a tall tree crosses the site during peak daylight hours, consider pruning away some branches. Removal of a single branch can make a big difference in the amount of light the bulbs receive and their subsequent flowering performance. Many early-flowering bulbs (like aconites and snow crocuses) look beautiful in woodland settings, but be sure the woodland is composed of deciduous trees that lose their leaves in winter. Closely spaced evergreens usually block out the light that the bulbs' leaves need to replenish the bulbs themselves.

Where shade is caused by a wall or fence, consider painting the fence white and mulching the soil with white landscape chips, which will increase the amount of light through reflection.

Drifts of daffodils can thrive on very lightly shaded slopes beside a woodland path, but most bulbs need sunnier spots for their best flowering.

Soil

Most bulbs—such as tulips, daffodils, dahlias, and garden lilies—thrive in a humus-rich soil. Humus is any well-decomposed organic matter, which is most easily added in the form of peat purchased as bales from garden centers. It is also readily available in the form of garden compost, well-decomposed animal manures, and leaf mold. Even those bulbs that thrive with their roots permanently submerged in water will grow contentedly in a humus-rich soil. Where the soil is too sandy or too heavy with clay, add humus. Sandy soil is generally a good growing medium because it has good drainage and is easily penetrated by plant roots. Humus gives the soil body, allowing it to hold nutrients and moisture.

While peat is available from garden centers, it can be expensive, so consider making a compost pile. If you don't have a compost pile, it's easy to start one. Simply build a wire bin in a corner of your property, and pile kitchen waste, animal manure, shredded leaves, garden waste, and any other kind of organic material into it. The compost will break down more quickly if the ingredients are layered. But even the most haphazard compost piles will yield a beautiful, dark, fluffy soillike material with high nutrient value as well as excellent soil conditioning benefits.

A heavy clay soil may need gypsum (a white, gritty, powdery substance) in addition to humus. Gypsum can be purchased from garden centers.

Bulbs perform best in soils with a pH that is neutral or near neutral (ideally between 5.5 and 7.3 on the pH scale). Soil that is too alkaline (as in desert areas) or overly acidic (as in forested, rainy areas) will

Collect leaves onto a tarp to make nutritious leaf mold, a type of humus that is a valuable soil conditioner.

inhibit the bulbs' growth. If you are unsure of your soil's pH balance, have it tested by a soil laboratory. Forms and mailing bags can be obtained from garden centers and local county agents. After the soil sample has been analyzed, you'll receive a computer printout that explains if there are any problems with your soil. If there is a pH imbalance, the printout will tell you precisely how to correct it; if nutrients are deficient, it will explain how to add them. Usually, a highly alkaline soil is improved by the addition of sulphur, and a highly acidic soil is corrected by the addition of lime. In extreme cases, it may be necessary to build a raised bed and truck in good topsoil.

Classes of Daffodils

To help gardeners make sense out of the profusion of daffodils, the Royal Horticultural Society has established a classification system that is recognized worldwide. The categories are:

Division 1: Trumpets (example, 'Spellbinder'—midseason). Long, conspicuous trumpets.

Division 2: Large-cupped (example, 'Fortissimo'—midseason). Short trumpets, largest flowers.

Division 3: Small-cupped (example, 'Birma'—early). Bull's-eye center is often intensely colored.

Division 4: Doubles (example, 'Tahiti'—late). Many layers of petals.

Division 5: Triandrus hybrids (example, 'Thalia'—midseason). Cluster-shaped flowers resembling a fuchsia blossom.

Division 6: Cyclamineus hybrids (example, 'Peeping Tom'—early). Small, rakish trumpet, swept-back petals.

Division 7: Jonquilla (example, 'Pipit'—midseason). Cluster-flowered, highly fragrant.

Division 8: Tazetta (example, 'Cragford'—early). Includes both hardy and non-hardy cluster-flowered forms. The tender varieties are known as paperwhites.

Division 9: Poeticus (example, 'Actaea'—late). Tiny cup with large bloom resembles a dogwood blossom.

Division 10: Species and wild forms (example, *Narcissus bulbocodium*—midseason).

Division 11: Split corona (example, 'Orangery'—midseason). The cup forms a wide, flat arrangement of petals, which are ruffled or star-shaped.

Division 12: Strictly speaking, this is a miscellaneous category containing varieties that do not fit elsewhere. But some bulb companies use it to group miniatures together, though most miniatures are simply small-flowered varieties from other classes (example, 'Tête-à-Tête'—early).

An abundant display of daffodils represents several of the classifications of the Royal Horticultural Sociey.

Double-Digging

Though most bulbs you purchase have enough reserves of energy to produce a good display the first season, to keep them coming back it may be necessary to have a well-prepared planting bed. Wherever the soil is poor, either too sandy or too clayey, then consider the sound practice of double-digging. This involves using string to stake out an area for planting and removing a layer of turf with a flat-bladed spade to expose the bare soil. Then dig down to twice the depth of the blade, and place the soil on a tarp. Add humus (such as compost, leaf mold, or peat moss), mixing it in thoroughly. Next, shovel the top layer of soil into the bottom and the bottom layer on top. Any fertilizer needed to provide nutrients and any lime (to control acidity) or sulphur (to control alkalinity), should be added before the two layers of soil are replaced.

The result will be a friable, nutrient-rich soil in which bulbs can thrive. The combination of breaking up the soil and adding humus will create a bed that is raised several inches above the original soil, and so to keep it in place, consider edging the bed with stone or wood. Be aware, too, that some bulbs (like foxtail lilies and crown imperials) demand extra good drainage to come back, and so will benefit from adding some fine gravel to the soil.

Double-digging involves piling two layers of soil onto tarps for soil improvement.

A beautiful clump of cactus-flowered dahlias (center) highlights a summer garden with montbretia (left), pansies, and sweet alyssum.

Classes of Dahlias

Dahlia flowers are shaped like pompons and can range in size from as large as dinner plates to as small as half-dollars. All will bloom continuously from early summer to fall frost. The main classifications are:

Cactus-flowered (example, 'Golden Heart'). Quilled petals.

Formal Decorative (example, 'Orange Julius'). Evenly spaced, rounded petals.

Informal Decorative (example, 'Envy'). Unevenly spaced rounded or twisted petals.

Pompon (example, 'Yellow Gem'). Miniature ball-shaped flowers.

Single (example, 'Bishop of Llandaff'). A single layer of petals forms flowers which closely resemble a daisy.

Planting

When you purchase bulbs, the package will generally explain how deep to plant them and what spacing to give them. For example, for trumpet daffodils you will be advised to plant bulbs 8 inches (20cm) deep from the base of the bulb and at least 4 inches (10cm) inches apart; for tulips the recommendation is usually 6 inches (15cm) deep from the base of the bulb and 4 inches (10cm) apart.

Normally, all bulbs are planted with the pointed side up, but some bulbs (like anemones) have irregular shapes, and it can be difficult to tell the up end. Don't worry. Even if you plant a bulb upside down, it will still send out a shoot that grows up. By far the easiest way to plant bulbs in a small area is simply to use a trowel like a dagger and stab the blade down into the soil to the required depth. Lever back the handle so the blade makes a V-shaped hole and push the bulb to the bottom, pushing back soil to cover the bulb. For larger plantings it is easier to use a long-handled bulb planter. The easiest kind to use has a metal wedge which can be pushed into the soil with your foot, without bending, then levered to open a V shape in the soil.

A long-handled bulb planter saves time when planting bulbs in heavy soil.

Why Bulbs Fail to Come Up

Bulbs are generally quite easy to plant, and if you choose those that are recommended for your hardiness zone, you should have good luck. There are, however, a few conditions that may cause bulbs to fail:

1. They were planted too late in the autumn, allowing a severe cold spell to kill the bulbs before they had a chance to establish an adequate root system.

2. They were planted in too dry a soil. This inhibits root development and also allows a severe cold spell to kill the bulb.

3. Soil pH was too acidic (below 5.5 on the pH scale) or too alkaline (above 7.3 on the pH scale).

4. Poor drainage allowed standing water to rot the bulbs.

In loose soils—such as sandy soil—a bulb planter can be used. This is usually in the form of a metal cylinder with a handle. By pushing the cylinder into the soil you can pull up a plug of soil and place the bulb in the hole. A shake of the handle then releases the plug back into the hole, covering the bulb. In heavy soils, however, the soil does not dislodge from the cylinder easily, and you may find yourself wasting a lot of time pushing the soil out of the cylinder with your fingers.

A short-handled bulb planter will save time when planting bulbs in loose soil.

How Deep to Plant?

For bulbs featured in "The Most Beautiful Bulbs to Grow," the correct planting depth is given for each variety of bulb. Most bulbs are quite forgiving; if you miss by a few inches either way the bulb will usually adjust to its planting depth, sending out a longer than usual flower stalk if planted too deep and a shorter stalk if planted too shallow. However, there are a few exceptions. Bearded irises are the most critical bulbs to plant correctly, since they require rather unusual conditions for proper growth. Like a boat floating on water, two-thirds of the bulb should be submerged in soil and a third exposed to sunlight, since bearded irises like their bulbous parts to bake in the sun.

Planting through Turf

Some bulbs—especially daffodils and colchicums—will grow through turf to flower, but tulips and hyacinths have difficulty competing with grass. To successfully grow bulbs in grass, you must prepare a special bed for them. Use a spade to slice through the turf to a depth of 2 inches (5cm), cutting a rectangle at least 18 inches (45cm) wide and 3 feet (90cm) long. Carefully roll back the turf to expose the subsoil and dig down at least 12 inches (30cm), placing the soil on a tarp. Fluff up the original soil and add humus if necessary, together with some high-phosphorus fertilizer. Then replace 6 inches (15cm) of the soil and on top of this improved soil place your bulbs in an informal pattern. Finally, fill up the bed and fold back the turf to cover the planting site.

For extremely large bulb plantings, it is advisable to use a mechanical auger. This has a screw end that quickly grinds into the earth, leaving a pile of soil to one side. Pop in the bulb and kick the soil back into the hole. Using an auger, it is possible for one person to plant 500 bulbs in a day.

When planting a formal bed, it is best to have an even spacing between bulbs, and the easiest design to plant is a diamond pattern. Stretch strings to mark the rows and after planting the first row make sure the second row is offset equidistant to the bulbs in the previous row. This will help create an even, regular pattern.

For a planting that appears naturalized, where you want the bulbs to look like they have planted themselves, lightly scatter the bulbs over the prepared bed and plant them more or less where they fall.

Below, top: Peel back sod to plant bulbs in turf.
Below, bottom: Then space the bulbs evenly in the soil.

Some bulbs are vigorous enough to grow through turf. However, the soil below the turf must not be compacted. For a planting through turf, peel back a section of turf, fluff the soil up with humus, then roll the turf back into position so it appears as it was.

Right: Use a lawn mower to shred leaves for making leaf mold. Below: Bone meal is a beneficial bulb fertilizer.

Fertilizing

If you want your bulbs to flower every year, and especially if you want them to multiply, you will need to feed them. Small bulbs—aconites, snowdrops, and snow crocus, for example—are extremely efficient at extracting all the nutrients they need from leaf litter or decaying mulch. However, large bulbs such as daffodils, hyacinths, and tulips generally need feeding twice a year: in the spring before the plants bloom and again in autumn, after the first frost. If you only have time to fertilize once, then do it in autumn.

The three most important plant nutrients are nitrogen, for green leaves; phosphorus, for healthy roots and flowers; and potash, for overall vigor and resistance to disease. On fertilizer packages, these are shown as percentages, such as 5-10-5, with the first number representing nitrogen, the second phosphorus, and the third potash. For bulbs, phosphorus is the most important nutrient; it is plentiful in bone meal and super phosphate. General-purpose fertilizers with a high middle number are very good for bulbs.

Leaf mold is such a good soil conditioner for bulbs that it is worth making your own if you have access to a lot of leaves. Simply rake leaves onto a tarp and drag them to a pile where they can be shredded with a lawn mower. Then dump the shredded leaves into a bin made with chicken wire. Shredded leaves will break down within six months and add a valuable, nutrient-rich, spongy humus to the soil.

Weeding

Bulbs have great difficulty competing with weeds, so it is vital to keep your bulb plantings weed-free. If your bulbs are in shade, mulch the soil surface with shredded leaves or pine needles; if your plantings are in an exposed rock garden, then mulch with gravel. Mulch bulbs planted in open beds and borders with wood chips, grass clippings, or shredded pine bark.

Be careful when pulling weeds that you do not disturb the bulbs. Aggressive weeds like dock or dandelion have long taproots with lots of feeder roots that can lift bulbs clear of the soil if they are pulled carelessly. Use a narrow, forked weeding tool to dig deep down beside stubborn weeds so the weed root comes up clean without clods of earth and adjacent bulbs attached. Delegate all weeds to the compost pile. Always tackle weeds *before* they have a chance to set seed.

Above: Add mothballs to tulip beds to repel rodents. Below: Use wire mesh to create a squirrel-proof barrier.

Pests and Diseases

Flowering bulbs are remarkably free of pests and diseases. Indeed, many bulbs (daffodils and hyacinths) have poisonous parts that deter foraging animals and insect pests from attacking them. Rodents that can burrow into the soil and eat bulbs underground are the worst pest problem for bulbs. I protect my vulnerable plantings by sprinkling rodent repellent flakes or mothballs among the bulbs when I plant them and then by sprinkling more flakes on top of the soil in subsequent years, though if you have young children who are likely to put things from the ground into their mouths, this may not be a good option for you. A cover of chicken wire further protects tulips and crocus from squirrels, who dig up and eat the bulbs.

Deer are especially fond of tulips and irises. If you cannot fence these animals out of your garden, then consider using a long-lasting deer repellent like "Hinder" or "Ropel," both of which are odorless to humans, but make the leaves of ornamental plants unappetizing to deer, rabbits, and groundhogs. These repellents are applied as a spray that is absorbed by the plant's tissues so that the entire plant becomes protected; one application can last up to three months.

Mites, aphids, and thrips are the principal insect spoilers of bulbs. Infested plants exhibit a lackluster appearance or show flower deformities. Aphids colonize the emerging shoots and can be blasted away with a strong spray of water. Mites are microscopic and can be detected by fine cobwebs among the leaves. They are difficult to control without the use of an insecticidal spray designed specifically to control mites.

For other problems, refer to the plant descriptions in the "The Most Beautiful Bulbs to Grow" chapter of this book. For example, there are disease-resistant lily varieties that combat fungus and bacterial disease.

These potatolike dahlia tubers are ready for dividing and winter storage.

Propagating Bulbs

Most bulbs reproduce themselves by several ingenious methods. Almost all bulbs can be propagated from seed, but this is usually slow and the results can vary. Seed propagation is used mostly by breeders and requires plenty of patience; it can take up to seven years for a bulb to bloom. Then the breeders evaluate hundreds of seedlings, seeking a variation that might be valuable in creating new varieties. Seed propagation is considered sexual propagation because it involves pollination between two different plants in the manufacture of seed.

Other forms of reproduction—such as division—are known as asexual. Asexual reproduction does not involve the production of seeds, nor is pollination required. The bulb simply divides, and it is this method that most bulbs employ to increase their numbers quickly.

Many bulbs (like daffodils) will divide naturally in a fertile soil, to double and triple in quantity each season. Others (like gladiolus) produce bulblets in the soil, which can be collected and planted elsewhere. Many lilies have a third method of reproduction, bulbils, which are formed along the upper part of the stem, in the leaf axils.

Daffodils are ready for dividing when the leaves fade and collapse.

Division

After one season of growing and flowering, most bulbs will start to divide or produce bulblets that can be removed from the mother bulb. Division is healthy for daffodil bulbs, which crowd each other after they multiply. Just dig them up and carefully separate the smaller bulbs from the sides of the mother bulb, and replant where you want them to grow. The larger bulbs (usually half the size of the mother) will be capable of flowering the next season, but the smaller bulbs may need an extra season to flower.

Dahlia tubers can be dug after the leaves die down in autumn. Start by washing the soil from them. When they are clean of soil, the tubers can be easily separated into clumps; each clump is capable of producing a new dahlia the following season. Dahlia tubers should be dried and stored in a well-ventilated, frost-free location, preferably nestled on a layer of moist peat.

Iris rhizomes sit close to the earth's surface, with their tops visible, so it's easy to see when a clump has become too large and needs to be divided. Simply dig up the clump and wash the roots clean. Then separate the rhizomes so that each has a crown of leaves. Cut the leaves about 4 inches (10cm) above the rhizomes and replant. Cutting the leaves ensures that each rhizome will stay anchored in the soil. Otherwise, the wind can catch the broad leaves like a sail and uproot the rhizome.

Bulbs should be divided by using a garden fork and prying up the soil as if you were lifting potatoes. Use the fork to gently raise the bulbs from the earth, then divide them.

Right: Clumps of daffodil bulbs ready for division. Below: Divided bulbs can be planted using a bulb planter.

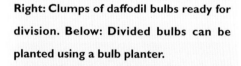

Dividing Bulbs and Remembering Where They Were Planted

How often have you wanted to divide bulbs but forgot where they were after the foliage died down? A good way to keep track is to press different colored golf tees into the soil among the foliage, making a note of which color represents which variety. Then, when the foliage has disappeared and the bulbs can be lifted, you can easily identify their location by the golf tees. Also, if you wish to fertilize your bulbs in autumn, the golf tees will help you determine where to place the fertilizer.

Bulblets

Gladiolus corms are examples of bulbs that produce small pea-size bulblets around the base of the mother bulb. Simply dig up the bulb in autumn after the leaves have started to turn brown, and rub the bulblets over a paper bag. They will drop away from the mother bulb with ease. Grade the bulbs by size since pea-size bulblets are unlikely to bloom the next season, while those the size of a quarter or larger are likely to flower. The pea-size bulblets will need to "size-up" for a season; this is best done by storing them over the winter and planting them in a special nursery bed after frost-danger in spring.

These gladiolus corms are perfect examples of mother bulbs with cormlets ready for division.

Bulbils

Some lilies (particularly 'Turk's Cap') will produce both bulblets (small bulbs around the mother bulbs) and bulbils (small black objects located in the leaf axils). Both the bulblets and the bulbils are an excellent source of new flowers, and their progeny will be identical to the mother plant. Often bulbils will drop from the mother plant with a root already breaking through. You can either pot these up in summer, or plant them in a special nursery bed to size-up. Flowering sometimes occurs the second season after planting.

Seed Starting

With a few exceptions, it can take years for bulb varieties to bloom from seed. Also, the

results from seed-grown bulbs—especially daffodil and tulip hybrids—can be highly variable, if not downright disappointing. Seeds may produce variations of the mother plant. Allowing bulbs to set seedpods can deprive the bulb of sufficient

energy to bloom again. However, there are some flowering bulbs that can produce spectacular results the first year from seed—sometimes producing larger flowers than bulbs—and usually at less cost. These include the 'Nonstop' tuberous begonias, 'Redskin' dahlias, 'Mona Lisa' anemones, 'Tropical Rose' hybrid cannas, and 'Bloomingdale' hybrid ranunculus. The seed-starting conditions for each of these bulbs vary considerably. Before starting any bulb from seed ask the supplier for specific

growing instructions. For example, the seed of 'Nonstop' begonias is tiny and must be surface-sown onto a peat-based potting soil in a seed-starting tray. A heating mat under the seed tray is advisable to maintain a soil temperature of at least 70°F (21°C), and the seed tray may need to be enclosed in a plastic bag to maintain a moist environment. When the seedlings have emerged and are large enough to handle, they can then be transferred to individual pots to reach transplant size, usually 4 inches (10cm) in height. The time needed from seed to transplant size for 'Nonstop' begonias can be 10 to 12 weeks. For best results, it's generally advisable to grow bulb varieties from the bulbs themselves.

Landscaping
with Bulbs

Opposite: Keukenhof bulb garden, near Amsterdam, presents a variety of bulbs to create a colorful landscape.

Mixed tulips in company with grape hyacinths make a decorative and colorful border for the edge of a lawn.

Different bulbs offer different landscaping opportunities. In general, summer-flowering bulbs tend to be taller than spring-flowering bulbs. Although there are some notable exceptions, most bulbs provide a relatively short, sensational burst of color. Because bulbs must be left in place for the leaves to die down, the best way to use them in the home garden is as fillers in mixed beds and borders, or naturalized in areas where they can be left undisturbed. Many parks and bulb gardens effectively use bulbs in massed beds. But the bulbs are usually dug up as soon as the flowers fade, and replanted every year—an expense and chore the average home gardener likes to avoid.

Some bulbs that will provide continuous color all summer until fall frost include dahlias, cannas, tuberous begonias, and caladiums. These are all tender and generally must be lifted and stored indoors during the winter. The following pages include some tips on the most popular ways to landscape with bulbs.

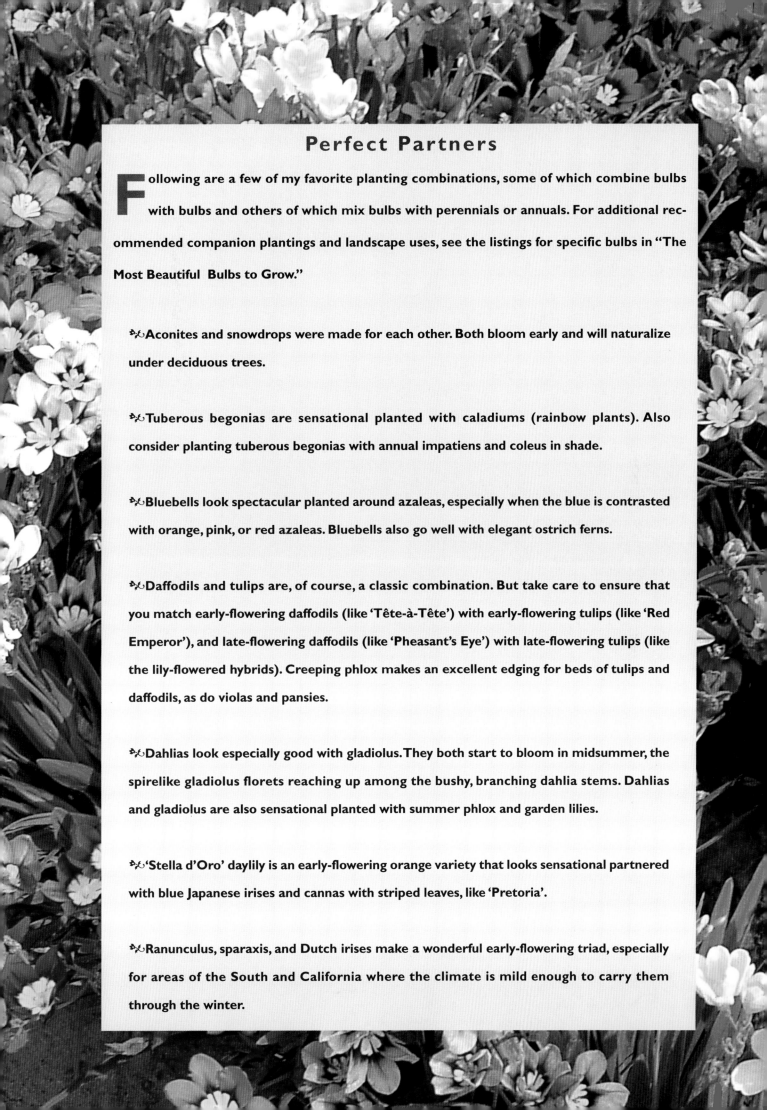

Perfect Partners

Following are a few of my favorite planting combinations, some of which combine bulbs with bulbs and others of which mix bulbs with perennials or annuals. For additional recommended companion plantings and landscape uses, see the listings for specific bulbs in "The Most Beautiful Bulbs to Grow."

❧Aconites and snowdrops were made for each other. Both bloom early and will naturalize under deciduous trees.

❧Tuberous begonias are sensational planted with caladiums (rainbow plants). Also consider planting tuberous begonias with annual impatiens and coleus in shade.

❧Bluebells look spectacular planted around azaleas, especially when the blue is contrasted with orange, pink, or red azaleas. Bluebells also go well with elegant ostrich ferns.

❧Daffodils and tulips are, of course, a classic combination. But take care to ensure that you match early-flowering daffodils (like 'Tête-à-Tête') with early-flowering tulips (like 'Red Emperor'), and late-flowering daffodils (like 'Pheasant's Eye') with late-flowering tulips (like the lily-flowered hybrids). Creeping phlox makes an excellent edging for beds of tulips and daffodils, as do violas and pansies.

❧Dahlias look especially good with gladiolus. They both start to bloom in midsummer, the spirelike gladiolus florets reaching up among the bushy, branching dahlia stems. Dahlias and gladiolus are also sensational planted with summer phlox and garden lilies.

❧'Stella d'Oro' daylily is an early-flowering orange variety that looks sensational partnered with blue Japanese irises and cannas with striped leaves, like 'Pretoria'.

❧Ranunculus, sparaxis, and Dutch irises make a wonderful early-flowering triad, especially for areas of the South and California where the climate is mild enough to carry them through the winter.

An Informal Border of Bulbs for Spring and Summer

This design shows only spring- and summer-flowering bulbs featured in this book; however, I encourage you to mix in some of your favorite spring and summer perennials. At Cedaridge Farm, we use these bulbs in company with perennials such as low creeping phlox and tall summer phlox, red-hot poker, purple coneflowers, and black-eyed Susans. For areas with mild winters, consider also planting drifts of ranunculus and sparaxis in the foreground.

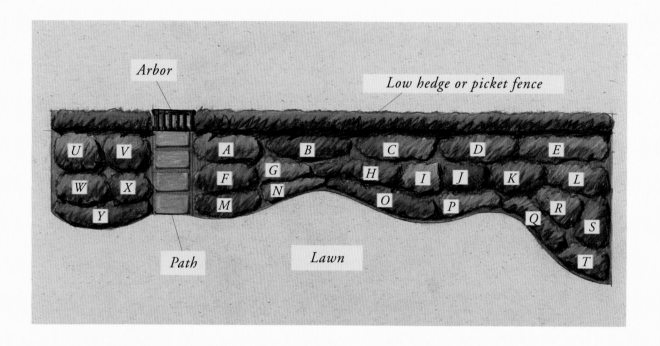

A 'Star Gazer' Oriental lily

B 'Mixed Colors' gladiolus

C 'The President' canna

D Dinnerplate dahlia

E Turk's cap lily (Lilium lancifolium)

F Dutch iris (Iris hollandica)

G Blackberry lily (Belamcanda chinensis)

H Naked lady (Lycoris squamigera)

I Foxtail lily (Eremurus elwesii)

J 'Mixed Colors' Asiatic lily

K Crown imperial (Fritillaria imperialis)

L 'Stella d'Oro' daylily

M Praestens tulip 'Fusilier'

N Bluebell (Endymion hispanicus)

O 'Professor Einstein' large-cupped daffodil

P Colchicum autumnale

Q 'Princeps' Greigii tulip

R 'Sapphire' bearded iris

S Leucojum aestivum 'Grayvite Giant'

T Hyacinth 'Delft Blue'

U 'Gudoschnick' Darwin hybrid tulip

V 'Caesar's Brother' Siberian iris

W 'Red Magic' daylily

X 'Beverly Sills' Iris × germanica

Y 'Mixed Colors' crocus

Beds and Borders

Beds are islands of soil surrounded by paving or lawn, while borders usually have a wall, fence, or hedge behind them. Beds are generally oval, rectangular, or kidney-shaped; borders are usually rectangular, often with a wavy edge in the front. The most successful beds and borders are raised above the surrounding soil by stones or landscape ties to improve drainage. The most colorful beds contain an assortment of spring- and summer-flowering bulbs. For maximum interest, I add perennials and annuals to mixed bulb plantings. Pansies and forget-me-nots are especially good partners for spring-flowering daffodils and tulips. Impatiens and coleus combine well with shade-loving, summer-flowering caladiums and tuberous begonias. You might want to think about creating a specific color theme, for example, a concentration of pinks, blues, and purples for a cool color harmony; and an emphasis on reds, yellows, and oranges for a hot color harmony.

This coastal garden in Oregon features a fine collection of dahlias in a perennial border at the edge of a lawn.

An Informal Island Bed of
Winter-Flowering Bulbs

In this design, I have used four early-flowering shrubs to provide some height and added interest. This kidney-shaped bed could also be effective encircling a tree, particularly a white birch or paper-bark maple, both of which have decorative winter bark. The bed should be mounded in the middle to facilitate drainage. For extra variety, you may want to include some perennial Lenten roses in the center and some primroses and carpet phlox around the edge.

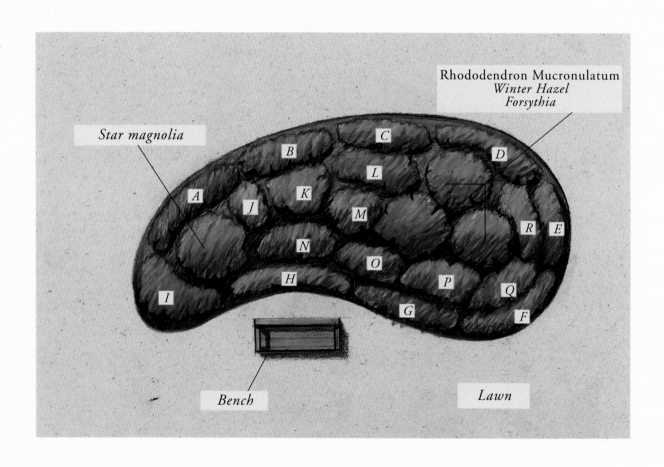

A	*Blue snow iris* (Iris reticulata)	J	*Aconites* (Eranthis hyemalis)
B	*Yellow snow iris* (Iris daenfordi)	K	*'Plaisir' Greigii tulip*
C	Crocus tomasinianus *'Ruby Giant'*	L	*'The First' Kaufmanniana tulip*
D	Crocus chrysanthus *'Bronze Beauty'*	M	Arum italicum
E	*Siberian squill* (Scilla sibirica)	N	Crocus flavus *'Yellow Mammoth'*
F	Crocus vernus *'Mixed Colors'*	O	*Spring-flowering cyclamen*
G	*Glory of the snow* (Chionodoxa lucida*)*		(Cyclamen coum)
H	*'Tête-à-Tête' daffodil*	P	*'Snowdrop'* (Galanthus elwesi)
I	*Grecian windflower*	Q	*'February Gold' daffodil*
	(Anemonde blanda)	R	Ornithogalum nutans

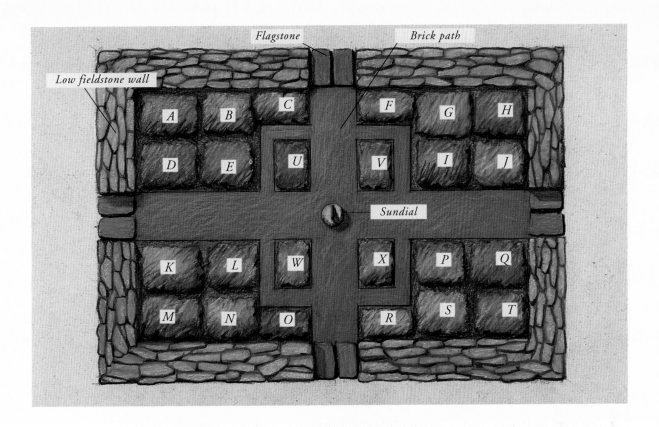

Flagstone

Brick path

Low fieldstone wall

Sundial

A Formal Tulip Garden

This rectangular plot is basically a quadrant design that is defined by a low stone wall and intersected by brick paths. In this particular scheme, each of the four planting areas features a different color harmony. For added interest, the borders of the paths can be planted with any low-growing edging plant, such as pansies, violets, or forget-me-nots. The sundial at the center of the garden serves as a focal point; a birdbath, small sculpture, or other accent would work as well. This design can be made more formal with the addition of dwarf boxwood hedges used as a border in place of the wall. At Cedaridge Farm, we plant the space with herbs after the tulips have faded.

A   'Ballade' lily-flowered tulip

B   'Burgundy' lily-flowered tulip

C   'Maytime' lily-flowered tulip

D   'Mariette' lily-flowered tulip

E   'White Triumphator' lily-flowered tulip

F   'Oxford' Darwin hybrid tulip

G   'Striped Apeldoorn' Darwin hybrid tulip

H   'Ad Rem' Darwin hybrid tulip

I   'Golden Apeldoorn' Darwin hybrid tulip

J   'Gudoshnick' Darwin hybrid tulip

K   'Arabian Mystery' triumph tulip

L   'Queen of the Night' triumph tulip

M   'Garden Party' triumph tulip

N   'Orange Wonder' triumph tulip

O   'Attila' triumph tulip

P   'Estelle Rijnveld' parrot tulip

Q   'Flaming Parrot' parrot tulip

R   'Orange Favorite' parrot tulip

S   'Karel Doorman' parrot tulip

T   'Fantasy' parrot tulip

U   'Angelique' late double-flowered tulip

V   'Nizza' late double-flowered tulip

W   'May Wonder' late double-flowered tulip

X   'Mount Tacoma' late double-flowered tulip

Rock Gardens

Rock gardens need not be large to look attractive. They are a perfect place to display spring-flowering bulbs, especially the miniatures such as Kaufmanniana tulips, 'Tête-à-Tête' daffodils, snow iris, and snow crocus. The best rock gardens include a water feature, such as a small waterlily pool, or a waterfall that spills water from one pool to another. You don't need an existing stream to do this since an inexpensive recirculating pump will keep the water in constant motion. My favorite rock gardens also feature some dwarf evergreen conifers, dwarf perennials—especially alpines like bellflowers—and some tufted ornamental grasses for added interest.

Naturalizing

I think one of the most uplifting sights in all of nature is a colony of flowering bulbs, especially in unexpected places. I immensely enjoy hiking and have a vivid memory of seeing miles of white avalanche lilies (*Erythronium montanum*) growing among the last patches of snow on the slopes of Mt. Rainier in Washington. At the other end of the world, I have marveled at the sight of pokerlike bulbocodiums stretching as far as the eye could see across sparse grassland near Cape Town, South Africa. When a plant is capable of establishing a self-perpetuating colony, as in the wild, the effect is called "naturalizing" or "perennializing." Daffodils are the easiest bulbs to naturalize and can cover acres of meadow and thin woodland. Other bulbs can be naturalized on a smaller scale. Some of the best include aconites, anemones, Spanish bluebells, colchicums, naked ladies, flag iris, snowdrops, and species tulips such as *Tulipa tarda* and *T. kaufmanniana*.

Naturalized Spanish bluebells in woodland at Winterthur garden, Delaware, lend a wild flavor to the scene.

Perennial Tulips

Many of the species, or wild, tulips naturalize readily. These include varieties of Kaufmanniana, Greigii, and Fosteriana tulips. Note, however, that bulbs of the larger-flowered hybrid varieties, such as the lily-flowered, double-flowered, and parrot tulips, have a natural tendency to split after the second season of flowering and produce "blind," or nonflowering, stems. Among the large-flowered tulips, the Darwin hybrids are the best for naturalizing. These should be planted extra deep (8 to 10 inches [20 to 25cm]) into a humus-rich, well-drained soil, and the beds should be fed twice a year with a high-phosphorus fertilizer—in spring before the bulbs bloom and again in autumn after the first frost. Also, if you are tempted to cut any of the flowers, leave at least two large leaves per stem to replenish the bulb.

Perennial Amaryllis

If you live in Zones 8–10, amaryllis may overwinter outdoors in your garden. These lovely flowers will tolerate light shade and look sensational planted in colonies under trees or in any sheltered part of the garden. Even gardeners in northern areas can flower amaryllis outdoors. Simply hold the bulbs in the vegetable bin of your refrigerator until after danger of frost has passed, then plant them outdoors. The bulbs will quickly break dormancy, send up big fat stems, and flower spectacularly. Of course, the bulbs must then be dug up and stored inside after frost kills the leaves in autumn. Amaryllis can also be grown indoors in a sunny window, where they make a picturesque part of many window displays. House-grown amaryllis thrive and bloom with relatively little fuss.

Children can be dwarfed by the enormous leaves of elephant ears.

A Touch of the Tropics

Many tender bulbs can introduce a tropical appearance to gardens, especially at the edges of a pond or in a sunroom. Although they will not overwinter where the ground freezes, tender bulbs are usually grown in pots that are temporarily sunk into the soil during the summer, then simply lifted and taken indoors during winter. The most exotic of these is elephant's ear (*Colocasia esculenta*), which produces massive heart-shaped leaves up to 6 feet (1.8m) long. Other tropical-looking tender bulbs include varieties of *Amaryllis, Agapanthus, Caladium,* and *Zantedeschia.*

Containers

When growing bulbs in containers, consider whether you want them for an extra-early indoor display or an outdoor display at normal flowering time; bulbs grown for early indoor display demand special treatment. A good potting soil, whether you are growing for outdoor display or indoors, will consist of one-third topsoil, one-third peat, and one-third sand.

For the best outdoor displays, try planting bulbs in window boxes and roomy whiskey half-barrels. Several varieties of bulbs grouped together make an especially appealing display, but the trick is to choose varieties that will bloom at the same time. Only experimentation will determine this. Because of the unpredictability of orchestrating the blooming of several varieties, it is generally more successful to devote one container to each variety, and mix the containers. If you want a rainbow display in one container, then choose a mixture of different-color hyacinths or a mixture of peony-flowered tulips.

Above: Sun-loving Persian buttercups grace terra-cotta planters. Below: Tuberous begonia in a barrel planter decorates a shady deck.

Above: A cluster of tulips is spaced in a pot for forcing. Below: Pots are sunk into a cold frame and covered to keep dark for 14 weeks.

To bloom indoors, most bulbs require a period of "cold treatment," but there are exceptions—amaryllis and paperwhite narcissus, for example. Just pot these bulbs and place them in bright light at room temperature and water. They will soon sprout and flower with little fuss. Daffodils and tulips, however, are examples of bulbs that demand at least thirteen weeks at a temperature below 48°F (9°C) in the dark, before they will bloom. You can get away with less time in the cold, but the bulbs will tend to be weak. First, choose pots with at least an 8-inch (20cm) mouth. Ensure that the pots have good drainage and set the bulbs so their tops are just below the soil surface. Water and set the pots in a

A display of hyacinths, tulips, daffodils, and an Easter lily basks in the sunroom at Cedaridge Farm.

cold frame, covering the tops of the pots with peat or wood chips to keep them dark. An old refrigerator, unheated garden shed, or cool basement will also do the trick. Keep the pots watered, and check them periodically to monitor their progress. First, the bulbs will develop a vigorous root system which should start to show through the drainage hole. Then the bulbs will send up green shoots. After the required thirteen weeks of cold treatment, move the pots to a room with bright light, and flowering should occur indoors within four weeks.

Drifts of daffodils planted at the edge of the lawn at Cedaridge Farm herald the beginning of spring.

Bulbs Through Four Seasons

Cedaridge Farm features bulbs through four seasons, starting in January and February with white snowdrops and yellow aconites that mingle their blooms with the saucer-shaped flowers of pink and white *Helleborus* (Lenten roses), a hardy perennial that makes a good companion for early bulbs. They are followed in March by drifts of snow irises *(I. reticulata)* and yellow crocus *(C. flavus)* that create a charming yellow-and-blue color contrast. These will all bloom before the last snowfalls of winter.

Peak flowering of daffodils occurs the last week of April, with miniature yellow 'Tête-à-Tête' leading the pack, lemon-colored 'Spellbinder' dominating the main display, and 'Pheasant's Eye' flowering late, to provide a good six weeks of continuous color from daffodils. Blue grape hyacinths are planted among the daffodils in another startling yellow-and-blue color harmony, while hyacinths in mostly blue, pink, and apricot form colonies under birch trees, where they fill the air with their wonderful, uplifting fragrance.

Tulips steal the show the first week of May, when we also have good overhead color from azaleas, dogwoods, crabapples, redbuds, and other early-flowering trees. Because we like to maintain an old-fashioned appearance we favor 'antique' tulip varieties like the bicolored yellow-and-red 'Keizerskroon' (which dates back to the 1700's), and wild species tulips, especially yellow *T. tarda*, red *T. praestens* and pink *T. bakeri*. Many of these species tulips are planted among clumps of 'Barnhaven' primroses, a tough strain developed in Oregon, which has cold-hardiness, plus good drought- and heat-tolerance. We also favor tulips planted as mixtures, particularly in lightly shaded locations

where they last several days longer than when planted in full sun. We favor 'hot' color groupings where red, orange, and yellow are the predominant colors, because so many other perennial plants at that time of year are 'cool' colors, such as pink and blue.

Along the stream banks at Cedaridge Farm, blue Siberian iris follow displays of daffodils and tulips.

After tulips have faded from the garden, the next big show of bulbs is from bearded irises (*I.* × *germanica*), which are mostly mixed in with major perennials such as herbaceous peonies, oriental poppies, and roses. Bearded irises are a wonderful bulb group to follow tulips since their color range is extensive and the flowers spectacularly big. Bearded irises like full sun and good drainage, so we have them planted in the open on sloping ground, but other irises like boggy ground, so we have a collection of these along a stream and in an area we call the swamp garden. Yellow flag iris (*I. pseudacorus*) and blue Siberian iris (*I. siberica*) are wonderful grouped together because the yellow and blue are such an appealing color combination. Japanese iris (*I. ensata*) bloom later in shades of blue and purple, and we like to partner them with yellow 'Stella d'Oro' daylilies to continue the yellow-and-blue theme.

The main summer display from bulbs comes from gladiolus and dahlias. These are so important to the summer garden that they have a large bed all to themselves at the edge of a spacious meadow. Gladiolus and dahlias predominate in 'hot' colors, which

look even more dramatic under a glaring summer sun, and so we deliberately concentrate on planting strong reds, bright yellows, hot pinks and blazing oranges.

A bed of gladiolus shines through the mist on a summer's morning at Cedaridge Farm.

We know it's midsummer when our naked ladies (*Lycoris squamigera*) bloom. We have them planted as colonies in all the perennial beds, especially in sunny locations like the cottage garden. Their pink trumpets rise above low-growing annuals such as nasturtiums and petunias, but their finest moment is when seen against a sheet of blue morning glories on fences in the background.

We are not fond of cannas, the tall gladioluslike plants with enormous upright leaves that remind me of banana trees, since they seem out of place in our farm setting. However, there is one place on the property where they excel—in our swamp garden.

We adore the variety 'Pretoria' (also known as 'Bengal Tiger') for its handsome striped leaves that look sensational when backlit. Cannas are grouped close to colonies of swamp hibiscus, making a good complement to the huge dinner-plate-size flower of the hibiscus. Likewise, 'Pretoria's' big, heart-shaped leaves are in perfect scale with the large-size cannas.

As summer slips into fall and a chill is felt in the early morning air, a series of autumn-flowering bulbs extends color even into frosty nights. These include the bright red *Amaryllis* and pink *Colchicums,* which are planted in drifts between clumps of azaleas and at the edges of waning perennial beds. More diminutive are colonies of pink cyclamen and various species of fall-flowering crocus, notably the blue saffron crocus. The pink of the colchicums and cyclamen and the blue of the crocus are a sensational color combination, especially seen against the variegated white leaves of *Miscanthus* grass, or poking through a carpet of dark leaves of black mondo grass. These are all featured in a small rock garden within sight of our breakfast room—which features bulbs in pots for precious color when the rest of the garden is dormant.

All things considered, flowering bulbs are an important component, of the plantings at Cedaridge Farm. With careful planning, they can provide twelve months of continuous color. Following are complete lists of bulbs showing their primary blooming season, so you can plan your own succession of color.

Amaryllis belladonna adds color to the fall flowering scene.

Bulbs for All Seasons

* An asterisk indicates a tender bulb suitable for frost-free (or nearly frost-free) outdoor gardens or indoor flowering in areas with severe winters.

** Double asterisks indicate bulbs used as annuals and either discarded after one season of bloom, or lifted in fall and stored over winter for replanting in spring.

Winter Flowering
(January, February, March)

* *Clivia miniata* (Kaffir Lily)

Eranthis hyemalis (Aconite)

Galanthus nivalis (Snowdrop)

* *Hippeastrum hybrids* (Amaryllis)

Iris reticulata (Snow Iris)

Crocus tomasinianus
(Snow Crocus)

Spring Flowering
(April, May, June)

* *Agapanthus africanus*
(Lily of the Nile)

Allium species
(Ornamental Onion)

* *Alstroemeria × hybridus*
(Inca Lily)

Anemone blanda
(GrecianWindflower)

* *Anemone coronaria*
(Florist's Anemone)

Arum italicum (Italian Arum)

* *Bulbinella floribunda*
(Yellow Cattail)

Camassia esculenta (Quamash)

Cardiocrinum giganteum
(Himalayan Lily)

Chionodoxa lucilae
(Glory of the Snow)

Convallaria majalis
(Lily of the Valley)

Crocus flavus (Yellow Crocus)

Crocus vernus (Dutch Crocus)

* *Cyclamen persica*
(Spring Cyclamen)

Eremurus himalaicus
(Foxtail Lily)

Erythronium hybrids
(DogtoothViolet)

* *Freesia hybrids* (Florist's Freesia)

Above: Cheerful yellow aconites shrug off late coverings of snow. Below: Spring-flowering 'Ballade' lily-flowered tulips and yellow crown imperials make good companions.

Summer-flowering varieties of oriental lilies are excellent for cutting.

Fritillaria imperialis
(Crown Imperial)

Fritillaria meleagris
(Snake's Head Fritillary)

Fritillaria persica (Black Fritillary)

* *Haemanthus katherinae*
(Blood Lily)

Hyacinthus orientalis
(Dutch Hyacinth)

* *Hymenocallis caroliniana*
(Spider Lily)

Ipheion uniflora (Starflower)

Iris fulva (Louisiana Iris)

Iris × germanica (Bearded Iris)

Iris hollandica (Dutch Iris)

Iris pseudacorus (Yellow Flag Iris)

Iris siberica (Siberian iris)

Iris versicolor (Blue Flag Iris)

Leucojum aestivum
(Summer Snowflake)

Leucojum vernus
(Spring Snowflake)

Muscari armeniaca
(Grape Hyacinth)

Narcissus species and hybrids
(Daffodil)

Ornithogalum species
(Star of Bethlehem)

* *Ranunculus asiaticus*
(Persian Buttercup)

Scilla campanula
(Spanish Bluebell)

* *Scilla peruviana* (Peruvian Squill)

Scilla siberica (Siberian Squill)

* *Sparaxis tricolor*
(Harlequin Flower)

Tulipa species and hybrids (Tulip)

* *Zantedechia aethiopica*
(Calla Lily)

* *Zephyranthes atamasco*
(Atamasco Lily)

Summer Flowering
(July, August, September)

** *Acidanthera bicolor*
(Peacock Flower)

** *Begonia tuberhybrida*
(Tuberous Begonia)

** *Caladium hortulanum*
(Rainbow Plant)

** *Canna generalis* (Canna)

** *Crinum × powellii*
(Crinum Lily)

Crocosmia × crocosmiiflora
(Montbretia)

** *Dahlia × hybrida* (Dahlia)

** *Eucomus comosa* (Pineapple Lily)

** *Gladiolus × hortulanus*
(Gladiolus)

Hemerocallis hybrids (Daylily)

Lilium hybrids (Garden Lily)

Lycoris squamigera
(Naked Ladies)

** *Polyanthus tuberosa* (Tuberose)

Sternbergia lutea
(Summer Crocus)

** *Tigridia pavona* (Tiger Flower)

** *Watsonia beatricis* (Bugle Flower)

Autumn Flowering
(October, November, December)

* *Amaryllis belladonna*
(Naked Ladies)

Arum italicum
(Italian Arum—berry display)

Colchicum autumnale
(Autumn Crocus)

Crocus sativus (Saffron Crocus)

Cyclamen hederiflorum
(Autumn Cyclamen)

* *Cyclamen persicum*
(Florist's Cyclamen)

Dahlia × hybrida (Dahlia)

* *Lycoris radiata* (Spider Lily)

Worsleya rayneri (Blue Amaryllis)

Where to Find Inspiration

Throughout the world, there are many places to visit to gain inspiration for using bulbs in a garden. For me, the most inspirational trip I ever took was to South Africa in their springtime, when thousands of varieties of bulbs bloom in the wild during a six-week period that usually begins in late August and early September. For the less adventurous, there are many exquisite gardens at home and abroad. Visit your local botanical gardens in spring to get ideas for bulb plantings for your own garden. Following is a sampling of a few truly sensational gardens devoted to bulbs.

'Jumblie' daffodils and helleborus are planted together near a lake at The Daffodil Mart, Virginia.

The Daffodil Mart

Brent and Becky Heath are a husband-and-wife team of growers and breeders who run a mail-order nursery from their farm in Gloucester, situated in the Tidewater area of Virginia. Their picturesque chalet-style home overlooks a tidal tributary on one side and acres of daffodils grown for evaluation and breeding on the other. Brent's grandfather moved to the area in 1900 and started a bulb-growing business when he discovered how readily daffodils grew in the area. Today, the enterprise has grown from a small business supplying local growers to a multinational company handling millions of bulbs supplying gardeners around the world. The garden is open in the spring, usually during the month of March, by appointment. Brent has spent forty-eight years in the business, and he is North America's leading expert on spring-flowering bulbs, especially daffodils.

Impressive tulip displays at Keukenhof Garden, Holland, flourish under the light shade of mature trees.

Keukenhof Garden

Seventy acres of flowering bulbs surrounding a large lake, 15,000 square feet (1,395 sq m) of greenhouses and gardens under glass, plus restaurants and gardens in a woodland setting surrounded by hundreds of acres of production fields drained by windmills—that is Keukenhof Garden, at Lisse, Holland, just a 30-minute drive from Amsterdam. It claims to be the greatest flower show on earth. Visited by more than one million people for six weeks from the end of March to the middle of May each spring, and sponsored by more than ninety of Holland's top bulb growers, who help pay for the planting of six million bulbs, it is truly worth making a special trip to see the garden—especially the first week in May, which is considered the peak bloom time. The value of Keukenhof is that you not only see lavish plantings on a scale unparalleled anywhere else in the world, but the gardens also present many good small-space bulb gardens, both formal and informal, so that the average homeowner can come away with a wealth of practical ideas that don't take an army of gardeners to implement.

Part of the spring tulip display at Lenteboden Bulb Garden, Pennsylvania, can serve as inspiration for your own garden.

Lenteboden Bulb Garden

Located on River Road, north of New Hope, Pennsylvania, Lenteboden garden is a miniature Keukenhof, with tiers of early-flowering bulbs planted in beds spreading down a hill through woodland, across a sunlit lawn, and onto a rock garden overlooking a tributary of the Delaware River. Hundreds of daffodil varieties appear after April 15, followed by hundreds of tulip varieties until mid May. Appointments aren't necessary. Visitors can wander the paths at their leisure, observe the latest varieties in full bloom, and just marvel at the spectacle. After touring the garden, you can fill out an order blank and have the bulb varieties shipped to your home at the proper planting time.

North American Bulb Fields

You do not have to travel to Holland to have the thrill of seeing hundreds of acres of tulips and other flowering bulbs in bloom. Tulips are a part of the agricultural economy of the Pacific Northwest (especially the Skagit Valley, midway between Portland and Seattle) and of Holland, Michigan. Both areas become a sea of color the first week of May, and each community hosts a week-long festival known as "Tulip Time." In Holland, Michigan, you will even see replicas of Dutch windmills decorating the tulip fields.

Later in the season, south of Portland, Oregon, there is no more beautiful sight than bearded iris blooming in the fields owned by the Schreiner family, and tuberous dahlias at Swan Island Dahlias (see "Sources" for addresses).

San Diego County, California, is a center of production for tender bulbs such as gladiolus, freesia, ranunculus, and Dutch iris. There is an especially large production area in Gardena, California, which is visible from the main highway running from Los Angeles to San Diego.

Production fields of Veldheer Tulip Farm, Holland, Michigan, with display gardens surrounding the windmill at rear.

The Most
Beautiful Bulbs
to Grow

Opposite: Trumpet lilies thrive in a cottage garden.

This encyclopedia of flowering bulbs contains those that are particularly beautiful for creative garden display and focuses mainly on hardy varieties. However, I've also included a representative selection of tender ornamental bulbs that will grow outdoors in frost-free areas or indoors in containers. Most of these can also be lifted in the winter and stored for replanting in the spring. Summer-flowering bulbs are highlighted with a ❧.

Cactus-flowered dahlias go well with the blue lily of the Nile.

Botanical Nomenclature

In this listing, plants are shown by botanical name, with their common name in parentheses. That is because many common names can refer to more than one type of bulb, creating much confusion (the common names autumn crocus, bluebell, and naked ladies, for example, apply to more than one plant). If you know a plant only by its common name, then look it up in the index to find the page where it is described.

Most wild species of bulbs (such as daffodils) have two parts to their botanical name: the first identifies the genus or family (*Narcissus*) and the second identifies a particular species within that family (such as *Narcissus bulbocodium*—the hoop petticoat daffodil). Sometimes there is a third part to the name, usually shown in single quotation marks, identifying a specific cultivar, or cultivated variety; for example, 'Golden Bells' is a free-flowering, extra-hardy selection of *N. bulbocodium*. Natural-occurring varieties are usually designated by the abbreviation "var." after the species name. If the variety is the result of hybridizing between two or more species, then there is an × in the name to signify its hybrid origin.

Be aware that botanical names are not always consistent because taxonomists (plant scientists responsible for maintaining botanical names) sometimes discover that there is some confusion internationally, or an error in naming, so they issue a name change. The most confusing example concerns bluebells. They are variously listed as *Scilla* and *Endymion*; the Dutch bulb industry still insists on calling them *Scilla*, while the botanists want them known as *Endymion*! In this book, you will find bluebells described under the name *Scilla*.

For each bulb mentioned in the descriptions that follow, the planting depth should be understood as measured from the base of the bulb.

❧Acidanthera bicolor
(peacock flower)

It's amazing to see this tall, elegant, spiky plant growing so thickly among wild grasses in South Africa; from a distance they appear as a sheet of shimmering water. The gleaming white flowers have a maroon eye, and resemble gladiolus. The irislike leaves stand stiffly erect. The plants grow to 3 feet (90cm) tall and flower in summer. Peacock flowers are not reliably hardy above Zone 7.

Plant the corms in the spring, 5 inches (12.5cm) deep, spaced 5 inches (12.5cm) apart. Choose a sunny position and soil with good drainage. Where severe freezing occurs during winter, lift the corms after frost kills the leaves and store them indoors for replanting in spring.

Peacock flowers make good tall accents for mixed borders and are popular cut flowers. They are exquisite when partnered with ornamental grasses, black-eyed Susans, Russian sage, gladiolus, and dahlias.

Above: Peacock flowers are prized for cutting. Left: Blue and white lily of the Nile cluster among trees.

❧Agapanthus africanus
(lily of the Nile)

Along the coasts of South and East Africa, I have seen lily of the Nile grow up and over barrier sand dunes, their mopheads echoing the color of the ocean. And in New Zealand, where they naturalize freely, I have seen them spread through woodlands as though they were bluebells! Clumps of straplike leaves produce long, slender flower stems topped by rounded flower clusters composed of blue or white trumpetlike florets, held on 5-foot (1.5m)-tall stems.

These magnificent summer-flowering, tender plants grow in sun or light shade, need a well-drained sandy or loam soil, and are highly drought-resistant. Plant the fleshy rhizomes 6 inches (15cm) deep, spaced at least 12 inches (30cm) apart. North of Zone 8 plant in the spring; in milder areas, plant the rhizomes in autumn.

These care-free plants are good for planting in small groups as tall accents or massed on sunny slopes for erosion control. They are sensational grown in pots outdoors, but need to be taken inside during the winter in areas where freezing occurs.

Allium giganteum
(giant onion)

Giant onions stand head and shoulders above perennials in a late spring border.

These gigantic relatives of onions and garlic grow large purple flower clusters up to about 5 inches (12.5cm) across, borne atop slender, 5-foot (1.5m)-tall, erect stems that emerge from a rosette of blue-green, arching, straplike leaves. Resembling giant drumsticks, they make a dramatic highlight for the late spring garden; they are best planted in groups of three or more. All parts of the plant have a mild oniony aroma.

There are many other species of *Allium* suitable for home gardens. Of particular interest are the 12-inch (30cm)-tall, spring-flowering *A. moly* (a yellow-flowered variety that can create a groundcover effect on sunny slopes) and the 3-foot (90cm)-tall, summer flowering *A. sphaerocephalum* (the purple-flowered drumstick onion). Also, don't overlook *A. schoenoprasum* (chives) as a pink, spring-flowering ornamental plant, famous as an edible herb commonly grown in kitchen gardens, but also beautiful in flower gardens.

Plant the baseball-size bulbs of *A.giganteum* in autumn in full sun in a humus-rich, well-drained sandy soil, pointed side up. Plant 8 inches (20cm) deep, spaced at least 8 inches (20cm) apart. Giant onions are best for Zones 4 to 8. The flowers sway in the wind and prefer a sheltered position. They are difficult to naturalize; the bulbs usually need replanting from new stock after the second or third season.

Use giant onions sparingly as tall accents for mixed perennial borders and for planting between low evergreen shrubs. While atttractive, too many giant onions can overwhelm a bed. Good flowering partners include bearded irises, peonies, and Oriental poppies. Allow the flower heads to dry and use them in dried flower arrangements as original accents sure to intrigue and please the eye.

A sunny slope is a good location for drought-resistant Inca lilies.

❧*Alstroemeria* × *hybrida*
(Inca lily)

What wild daylilies are to the meadows of North America, Inca lilies are to the waysides of Peru. The flowers resemble flocks of butterflies and bloom on plants that form clumps of sword-shaped leaves. Colors include orange, yellow, pink, apricot, and purple; most flowers have conspicuous black flecks in their throats. Inca lilies grow to 3 feet (90cm) tall and flower in the summer. The 'Ligtu Hybrids' are an especially good mixture.

These plants are not reliably hardy north of Zone 7. They prefer a well-drained loam soil in full sun. Plant dormant tubers in the spring, 4 inches (10cm) deep, spacing plants 12 inches (30cm) apart.

Inca lilies make good accents in mixed perennial borders and are perfect partners for lilies of the Nile. The plants will naturalize in mild-winter locations. They are useful for controlling soil erosion.

Grecian windflowers thrive in humus-rich soil around deciduous trees.

Anemone blanda

(Grecian windflower)

Native to the eastern Mediterranean, these diminutive plants grow just 4 inches (10cm) tall, but each star-shaped flower measures 2 inches (5cm) across. Many bulbs are needed to form conspicuous colonies. Grecian windflowers grow in shades of blue, rosy red, and pink, plus white and bicolors, and bloom at the same time as daffodils. The flowers are accented by bright yellow centers; the leaves are toothed, fernlike, and dark green. There is a similar species, called *A. apennina*, which bears blue flowers.

Plant the knobby corms in autumn, 5 inches (12.5cm) deep, spaced 2 to 3 inches (5 to 7.5cm) apart in sun or light shade in humus-rich loam or sand. The windflower is best for Zones 4 to 8.

Use these bulbs to create a carpet of color between taller spring bulbs such as tulips. Group them among rocky outcrops in rock gardens or establish naturalized plantings under ornamental deciduous trees such as crab apples and cherries. Plant in drifts of a single color or mix the colors. Good flowering partners include miniature daffodils such as 'Tête-à-Tête', early species tulips such as 'Stresa', and early-flowering perennials such as yellow primroses and pink fern-leaf bleeding hearts.

Anemone coronaria

(florist's anemone)

These Mediterranean wildflowers spangle the slopes of coastal meadows throughout Greece like rare and exotic jewels. The flowers resemble poppies with their vivid, silky petals and ring of powdery black stamens. Colors include red, pink, purple, blue, and white, plus bicolors. There are single-flowered types (such as 'De Caen') and semidouble types (such as 'St. Brigid'). The foliage is fernlike and toothed on 10-inch (25cm)-high plants. The flowers can measure up to 3 inches (7.5cm) across.

Autumn planting is recommended for Zones 7 to 10; elsewhere plant the bulbs in the spring since they are tender. They will not come back a second year in areas with severe winters unless they are planted in containers and taken indoors during freezes. Florist's anemones prefer full sun, but will tolerate partial shade if grown in a humus-rich, sandy, well-drained soil. Plant the corms 5 inches (12.5cm) deep, spaced at least 4 inches (10cm) apart. The corms are an irregular shape and it is difficult to tell which end is up. But don't worry, they will flower even if they are planted upside down.

Florist's anemone is best planted as an edging in a ribbon of mixed colors, or in colonies in beds and borders mixed with early perennials or other early bulbs. They are excellent for cutting and last well in water. 'Mona Lisa' is the cultivar used most by florists but only grows full size when it is started from seed. *Ranunculus* make excellent flowering partners.

Florist's anemones are good for edging paths in areas with mild winters.

Arum italicum
(hooded arum, Italian arum)

Arum is prolific as a woodland wildflower throughout Italy, especially along boggy stream banks. There are three stages of ornamental effect: when the arrow-shaped, mottled green-and-white leaves appear in autumn and remain through spring; when the hooded lime-green flower spathe appears early in spring; and finally when the spadix (the pokerlike protrusion inside the hood) turns into an arresting beacon of bright red berries.

Plant arum in the spring or autumn, in a lightly shaded position, such as under a deciduous tree. The soil should be fertile, humus-rich, and moist. If the soil under the tree is shallow or hardpan (a layer of hard subsoil or clay), consider creating a raised bed with a circle of stones. Mulch the soil with shredded leaves to keep it moist. Plant bulbs 5 inches (12.5cm) deep, spaced at least 12 inches (30cm) apart. Italian arum is best for Zones 5 to 9.

Arum is an excellent component of shade gardens and is effective when grouped in colonies among ferns and hostas. It does well in boggy soil. The glossy leaves, hooded flowers, and berries are all suitable for fresh arrangements but since they are poisonous, always wash your hands thoroughly after handling. Be warned that small children might be attracted to these bright berries.

Plant arum with helleborus (Lenten roses) for a good plant partnership.

Italian arum produces a striking berry display in late summer, after its leaves die down.

❧*Begonia* ×
tuberhybrida
(tuberous begonias)

Tuberous begonias bloom spectacularly when planted in light shade and a humus-rich soil.

The tropical plant family of begonias is one of the largest in the flowering king-dom. Most are native to South America, where they grow in rain-forest condi-tions, and are often misted from the spray of waterfalls or mountain fog. Begonias are possibly the most colorful flowering plant you can consider for a shady area. Although plants will not overwinter in northern gardens except under glass, the flat, round corms are easily stored indoors. The plants produce camellialike flowers up to 6 inches (15cm) across in a rich and varied color assortment that includes red, orange, pink, yellow, white, and bicolors. Flowering occurs throughout the summer. The leaves are also attractive, resembling angel's wings.

Plant the corms indoors in flats, in a peat-based potting soil, to get them sprouted. Then, when the plants are 4 inches (10cm) high and all danger of frost has passed, transfer them to the garden. In addition to a shady location, begonias demand good drainage and a cool soil, preferably loaded with humus. Water them regularly. Plant the corms 3 inches (7.5cm) deep, almost touching one another, to get them started. But when transferring them to the garden, space the corms at least 6 inches (15cm) apart.

Begonias are good for massing in raised beds around trees and along woodland paths. They are extremely beautiful grown as pot plants to decorate shady patios and decks, and are also attractive in hanging baskets and window boxes.

Bulbinella floribunda
(yellow cattail)

Yellow cattail looks like a yellow rocket shooting sky-ward. The plants resemble red-hot pokers and form clumps of slender, arching leaves. Yellow cattails flower in the spring.

This plant is not reliably hardy north of Zone 8. Plant the bulbs in autumn, 4 inches (10cm) deep, spaced 6 inches (15cm) apart, in a well-drained or moist soil.

Yellow cattails are best when planted as a colony on sunny slopes, in rock gardens, along stream banks, or as highlights in drought-tolerant landscapes.

Above: Indigenous to South Africa, yellow cattail covers hundreds of acres of boggy soil across sunny meadows. Left: Unlike most plants, rainbow plant leaves provide the color, while their small flowers are hidden.

Caladium
×
hortulanum
(rainbow plant)

There is hardly an area of tropical South America where rainbow plants are not abundant, mostly growing in boggy soil along rivers and in the rain forests. They are tender tropical plants that produce beautiful heart-shaped leaves in a rich assortment of colors. While it is the leaves for which they are grown, the plants do produce a cream-colored hooded flower spathe in the summer, though the flower is usually hidden among the leaves. No two leaves are exactly alike. Sometimes they are all one color, such as pink, white, or red, with prominent veins; at other times, the leaves are richly marbled or spotted to create a bicolor or tricolor effect. The plants do not normally exceed 2 feet (60cm) high, although there is a giant-leafed caladium, *Colocasia esculenta* (elephant's ear), that can reach 5 feet (1.5m) in height, with leaves equally as large.

Plant the bulbs in spring after the last frost, 4 inches (10cm) deep, and at least 12 inches (30cm) apart. Rainbow plants prefer light shade and a humus-rich loam soil, though they will grow in a moist, boggy soil. In areas where there is frost, lift the bulbs in autumn after frost has killed the leaves, clean the bulbs, and store them indoors in a dark frost-free area. About eight weeks before the last frost date in your area, pot and water the bulbs to force early sprouting so the plant provides a long foliage display.

For garden display, transplant the sprouted bulbs and use them as bold accents along stream banks, to encircle trees, or along the shady side of the house.

Camassia esculenta

(quamash)

Blue spires of quamash accompany creeping phlox in a rock garden, contributing their color and texture to the scene.

Quamash is native to the alpine meadows of the Pacific Northwest. Although all parts of the plant should be considered poisonous, the Indians had a way of cooking the bulbs so they could be eaten. The plants produce smooth, narrow, pointed leaves and tall, slender flower stalks. In early spring, the 3-foot (90cm)-tall stalks are topped by blue or white star-shaped flowers that form a spike.

Plant bulbs in autumn, 5 inches (12.5cm) deep in sandy, well-drained, humus-rich fertile soil in full sun. Space bulbs at least 4 inches (10cm) apart. The bulbs are pear-shaped and should be planted with the pointed end up.

Quamash is best grown in clumps with early-flowering perennials in mixed beds and borders. It looks good in rock gardens and combines particularly well with azaleas. Quamash is also good in meadow gardens and massed on sunny slopes. The flowers are suitable for cutting and make lovely indoor displays.

Cannas have an exotic tropical appearance, as shown here partnered with tender spider plants.

Canna ×
generalis
(Indian canna)

The word "Indian" in the common name refers to the West Indies, although most species come from South and Central America. Plants grow tall, strong stems with broad, banana-shaped bronze or green leaves and a flower spike of gladioluslike blooms in mostly red, pink, yellow, and orange. The cultivar 'Pretoria' not only has attractive orange flowers, but ornamental zebra-striped leaves. It is especially beautiful as a component of water gardens in company with swamp hibiscus.

Cannas tolerate poorly drained soil and high heat; the group called 'Water Canna' even thrives in shallow water. All cannas are somewhat tender and not reliably hardy above Zone 8. The large bulbs should be planted in the spring after danger of freezing temperatures is past. Plant them in a sunny position to a depth of 8 inches (20cm) and spaced at least 8 inches (20cm) apart. The bulbs are easily lifted and stored indoors during winter. In recent years, seed suppliers have offered a strain of cannas that will flower the first year from seed. Called the 'Tropic' series, the rose-colored species, 'Tropic Rose', won an All-America award. To germinate, the bullet-hard seeds must be soaked overnight in lukewarm water; start at least eight weeks before outdoor planting and transplant after danger of frost.

These plants make good tall accents for the back of mixed borders and the center of island beds, where low-growing, bushy plants like zinnias and marigolds can hide the bare lower portions of stem.

Cardiocrinum giganteum

(Himalayan lily)

This extremely tall-growing, spring-flowering bulb can reach 12 feet (3.6m) or more in height, and is topped with gorgeous trumpet-shaped white flowers with maroon throat markings. The heart-shaped leaves are bright green, heavily veined, and lustrous. Native to the rhododendron forests of northern India, there is nothing in all the bulb kingdom quite so majestic. Himalayan lilies are best for Zones 7 and 8, where the soil remains moist throughout the summer.

Plant the large pointed bulbs in autumn so the tip protrudes through the soil, spacing plants at least 3 feet (90cm) apart. They demand a humus-rich, acid soil with good drainage, and prefer a lightly shaded location. The main bulb will die after flowering, but not before it produces offsets that continue to live on. The flat, rounded seeds germinate reliably in a moist, peaty soil, but may take five to seven years to bloom.

Himalayan lilies make wonderful tall accents for woodland gardens, especially in the company of rhododendrons, primulas, hostas, and blue poppies. There are spectacular colonies of these plants in the botanical garden of the University of British Columbia in Vancouver. Gardeners outside the Pacific Northwest have been slow to try these amazing giants because they look so exotic and tender. However, I know of a plant growing in a sheltered woodland garden just south of Philadelphia, which has inspired me to try it in my Zone 6 garden at some time in the future. If these flowers can flourish outside the Pacific Northwest, their beauty can be spread around North America.

The tall Himalayan lily needs a sheltered location that offers light shade and humus-rich soil.

Chionodoxa luciliae
(glory of the snow)

Native to alpine meadows of Europe and Asia, glory of the snow has dainty, star-shaped blue flowers that emerge in early spring, soon after snowdrops and aconites appear. The cheerful flowers are held in loose clusters above narrow, smooth green leaves. There is also a rare pink variety, as well as a white one. Growing just 4 inches (10cm) tall, these plants can form extensive colonies that, from a distance, look like a pool of blue water.

Plant bulbs in autumn, 5 inches (12.5cm) deep in a sunny or lightly shaded location. Space at least 2 inches (5cm) apart in a humus-rich, well-drained soil. The bulbs are marble-size and should be planted pointed end up. Many bulbs are needed in order to make an impression, so buy them in multiples of fifty or a hundred. They will naturalize in Zones 4 to 8.

Plant glory of the snow under deciduous trees for a carpeting effect or as drifts among rocky outcrops. Partner it with miniature daffodils like 'Tête-à-Tête' and early-flowering species tulips like *Tulipa tarda*.

Glory of the snow masses on a slope in a lightly shaded woodland garden.

Clivia miniata
(Kaffir lily)

Kaffir lily's 12-inch (30cm)-wide flower clusters are composed of trumpet-shaped florets, mostly reddish orange with yellow throats. There is also a rare yellow variety. The leaves are dark green, arching, and straplike. Handsome, tender plants, Kaffir lilies are related to amaryllis. Though they will not overwinter outdoors north of Zone 9, they are popular as house plants. These spring-flowering plants grow to 2 feet (60cm) tall. Kaffir lilies are also known as Natal lilies.

Plant the baseball-size bulbs in autumn so that the neck protrudes just above the soil surface, spacing the plants at least 12 inches (30cm) apart. Give them a lightly shaded location and well-drained, humus-rich soil.

Kaffir lilies are sensational for edging woodland walks and shady slopes. They are perfect partners for palms, cycads, and tree ferns when grown outdoors. Kaffir lilies can also be grown in large outdoor or indoor containers. Choose pots that set off their bright blooms to advantage. Amaryllis make good indoor or outdoor companions.

Left: Kaffir lilies like a frost-free location, in light shade. Below: *Colchicum* will grow through turf.

✣ *Colchicum autumnale*
(autumn crocus)

The beautiful pink star-shaped flowers of autumn crocus appear in late summer on bare stems. The straplike leaves appear in spring, and disappear by the time the plants flower. I have seen colonies the size of a football field descending dry, grassy slopes in the Atlas Mountains of Morocco. The species has chalice-shaped flowers. The hybrid variety 'Waterlily' has flowers up to 4½ inches (11cm) across and resembles a pink waterlily.

Plant the bulbs in spring, 5 inches (12.5cm) deep in fertile, well-drained, sandy or loam soil, choosing a sunny location. Space at least 4 inches (10cm) apart. Like daffodils, the bulbs are toxic to animals and humans. Autumn crocus performs best in Zones 5 to 8.

These bulbs are lovely planted in colonies on sunny slopes and along paths, especially between shrubs. They are also ideal for rock gardens. In the summer, the bulbs can be dug up, cleaned of soil, and placed on a sunny window without soil or water, to miraculously bloom in autumn. Then they can be transferred to the garden to complete their normal life cycle.

Fragrant lily of the valley makes a durable, hardy ground cover in sun or shade.

Convallaria majalis
(lily of the valley)

Native to Europe, lilies of the valley are a source of the cherished and expensive perfume Muguet de Bois. In spring, masses of nodding, bell-shaped white flowers are clustered at the top of slender stems, which rise from a clump of spear-shaped leaves. There is a rare pale pink variety as well as a variegated form. The plants grow to just 6 inches (15cm) tall. Their aggressive rhizomes, called pips, form dense, weed-suffocating colonies.

Plant the rhizomes 2 inches (5cm) deep, 4 inches (10cm) apart in a sunny or lightly shaded location. The plants tolerate impoverished soil, provided drainage is good. Lily of the valley is hardy from Zones 3 to 8 and should be planted in autumn.

These bulbs make a good dense groundcover, especially for edging beds and along lightly shaded woodland paths. Lily of the valley is also suitable for growing in containers and cutting.

Crinum × powellii
(crinum lily)

I have seen crinum lilies with their gorgeous trumpet-shaped flowers growing wild throughout the Bahamas, flowering in spring. The predominant form resembles a white trumpet lily, although the plants are related to amaryllis. The pink-and-white striped species, *C. bulbispermum*, has been used to create the hybrid *C. × powellii*, which is available in two color forms, 'Alba' (white) and 'Roseum' (pink). The natural range of crinums extends south throughout Central and South America. They naturalize with ease wherever winters are mild, establishing handsome clumps with arching, straplike leaves. Crinums flower in the spring and can reach up to 3 feet (90cm) tall. They perform best in Zones 8 through 10, particularly in the Gulf states and California.

Plant the large bulbs in autumn, 8 inches (20cm) deep and at least 12 inches (30cm) apart, in well-drained sandy or loam soil in full sun or light shade. It is best if the long neck of the bulb extends just above the soil surface. In northern gardens, these plants can be grown in containers and moved indoors during winter.

Crinum lilies are superb accents in mixed borders, especially where drought-tolerance is important. They are excellent for naturalizing in mild winter areas, particularly near the coast. The long, strong stems make them good for cutting and showing in vases.

Crinum lilies need a frost-free location and full sun to form a colony like this.

*Crocosmia* × *crocosmiiflora*

(montbretia)

An aggressive wayside plant from South Africa, montbretia has escaped into the wild throughout the Pacific Northwest, especially along the coast where it helps to control soil erosion. The irislike plants produce sword-shaped and arching flower stems topped in summer with tubular florets arranged in a spike. Although they are reasonably hardy, the plants need protection in Zone 6, their northern limit. Montbretias grow to 3 feet (90cm) tall. Their colors include red, orange, and yellow.

Plant the corms in spring or autumn, 4 inches (10cm) deep and at least 12 inches (30cm) apart in well-drained soil.

Montbretia is a good accent for mixed borders, especially when combined with lily of the Nile, daylilies, and black-eyed Susans. This colony-forming bulb is a strong choice for meadow gardens.

Montbretia is a valuable summer-flowering bulb, mostly offered in orange and red.

Crocus vernus

(Dutch crocus)

Native to mountains surrounding the Mediterranean, the Dutch crocus is an early-flowering plant that bridges the gap between snowdrops and daffodils. The chalice-shaped flowers open out like waterlilies on bright, sunny days, to display rich orange stigmas. Colors include purple, white, and bicolors. A yellow species, *C. flavus*, is often included in mixtures of Dutch crocus to extend the color range.

There are several other good early crocus species known as snow crocus because they bloom a week or two ahead of the Dutch crocus, including *C. tomasinianus* (pale blue) and *C. chrysanthus* (which is rich in yellows). There are several autumn-blooming species, including *C. speciosus* (purple-flowered) and *C. sativus* (saffron). The leaves of all Dutch crocuses are narrow and pointed, with a silvery stripe down the middle. These plants grow just 4 inches (10cm) tall.

Plant corms of spring-flowering crocus in autumn; plant autumn-blooming species in the summer. Both types should be planted 4 inches (10cm) deep, spaced at least 2 inches (5cm) apart in well-drained, fertile soil. Dutch crocuses prefer full sun or light shade. The plants will naturalize freely in Zones 4 to 8. The bulbs are round and flattened, usually with a small point showing which end is up.

These bulbs are absolutely perfect for creating a colorful carpeting effect under deciduous trees, and are also useful for edging beds and borders. They are especially beautiful planted as drifts in rock gardens, where they combine very well with Grecian windflowers and Kaufmanniana tulips. Crocus are easily forced to bloom indoors in pots.

Even a light covering of snow will not deter crocus from flowering in early spring.

Cyclamen hederifolium
(hardy cyclamen)

Cyclamen are native mostly to the eastern Mediterranean, especially Greece, where they grow in thinly wooded areas. The hardiest cyclamen is *C. hederifolium* (also known as *C. neapolitanum*). It is suitable for Zones 4 to 8 and flowers in autumn. Plants grow just 4 inches (10cm) tall. They form colonies of heart-shaped, marbled leaves and purple flower stems topped by nodding flowers with swept-back petals. Cyclamen colors include red, purple, pink, and white. Hybrids of the tender *C. persicum* are known as florist's cyclamen. They make popular Christmas and Easter gift plants, but are unsuitable for growing outdoors, except in frost-free areas.

Plant corms in the spring, 4 inches (10cm) deep, spaced 4 inches (10cm) apart, in humus-rich, well-drained loam soil. Mulch the beds to keep the soil moist. Cyclamen will grow in the sun if the soil can be kept cool. Light shading and a high humus content, together with a mulch of shredded leaves, should keep the soil at a temperature suitable for cyclamen. The corms are round and flat, usually with protrusions indicating which end is up. A hardy spring-flowering species, *C. coum*, is available for autumn planting.

Cyclamen are excellent additions to shade gardens, especially when partnered with small ferns like Japanese silver fern. They are also effective planted as drifts in shady rock gardens and make exquisite potted plants.

Above: Cyclamen can grow through English ivy. Left: Cactus-flowered dahlia demands full sun.

❧ *Dahlia × hybrida*
(d a h l i a)

Dahlias are amazingly versatile plants, offering a rich assortment of colors. Varieties range in size from compact 12-inch (30cm) tall patio plants with daisylike blooms to dinner-plate-size dahlias on branching stems that grow up to 6 feet (1.8m) tall. The stems are succulent and hollow, and generally need staking. Leaves are bright green or bronze, and indented. Native to Mexico, dahlias are now such a complex group, they have been divided into specific classifications (see page 24).

These plants are tender and generally will not overwinter in the ground above Zone 7. The tubers are sausage-shaped and should be laid horizontally 3 inches (7.5cm) deep from their bases. Space the dwarf, compact varieties 12 inches (30cm) apart; tall kinds should be spaced at least 3 feet (90cm) apart. Plant dahlias in the spring after danger of frost is past, in fertile, humus-rich loam or sandy soil. Flowering is continuous until autumn frost, when the tubers can be dug up, cleaned of soil, and stored in a frost-free place through winter.

The dwarf, compact varieties are excellent for containers and massed bedding displays. The tall kinds can be used as accents in mixed beds and borders and for cutting. Dahlias are good partners for gladiolus.

Eranthis hyemalis

(winter aconite)

Though covered with snow, these aconites will continue to flower when the sun melts the ice.

Usually the first flowering bulbs to bloom in spring (even a day or two ahead of snowdrops), the iridescent yellow, buttercuplike flowers of winter aconite emerge from the soil with frilly green collars, followed by toothed dark green leaves. Aconites are native to the mountains of eastern Europe and Asia, where they carpet the slopes for miles. They readily naturalize in North America, self-seeding freely, especially in Zones 3 to 8.

The bulbs resemble dried raisins, and it is difficult to know which end is up. However you plant them, the shoots always emerge from the top. Plant the bulbs in autumn, 4 inches (10cm) deep, and space them at least 2 inches (5cm) apart. Give them a humus-rich soil and mulch with either shredded leaves or pine needles to keep the area weed-free. Store-bought bulbs may be overly dry and may need to be soaked in lukewarm water for an hour to freshen them up. Aconites like full sun but tolerate light shade, especially under deciduous trees.

After flowering, the plants form seed capsules with dark brown seeds that can be sprinkled onto bare soil. Press them into the upper soil surface and they will germinate and flower the second season. The greatest success with aconites is assured by digging up an established clump in early spring, shortly after flowering, and replanting it.

Best planted on a sunny bank or under deciduous trees to form colonies, aconites are also suitable for planting in drifts in rock gardens. They are especially pretty when combined with other early-flowering bulbs such as snowdrops, snow irises, and snow crocuses.

Foxtail lilies stand out like rockets against evergreen trees and a hedge.

Eremurus himalaicus
(foxtail lily)

Native to the deserts of Asia, foxtail lily has fleshy, smooth, sword-shaped leaves that resemble those of yucca. From the center of each rosette emerges a tall flower stem topped by a long, tapering cluster of star-shaped white flowers; the flower stalks can reach 6 feet (1.8m) tall. Foxtail lilies flower in late spring. There are also yellow-flowered and pink-flowered species, plus a hybrid mixture that includes orange. However, these species are more temperamental, less hardy plants.

A sandy, gravelly soil in full sun is essential to keep these high desert plants coming back. Plant the tuberous bulbs in autumn, 5 inches (12.5cm) deep, at least 2 feet (60cm) apart. The bulbs are shaped like an octopus, with a hard center and fleshy sausage-shaped roots extending out. Set the arms so they slant down or sideways, with the growing point just below the soil surface. It is best to make a special pit for foxtail lilies by digging a trench 2 feet (60cm) deep and filling it with a mixture of equal parts sand, gravel, and topsoil. In northern gardens, the plants need to be mulched for added protection. If a freeze follows a warming trend, protect the emerging flower stalk with a burlap or plastic covering. This plant grows best in Zones 5 to 8.

Because of their height, foxtail lilies make good accents in mixed beds and borders. They can be massed for a bold effect, or scattered throughout the garden to add a glittering quality. Foxtail lilies also make exquisite cut flowers. In the garden they make good partners for delphiniums.

Erythronium ×
hybrida 'Pagoda'
(dogtooth violet)

Species of *Erythronium* grow wild throughout North America, although most of the wild species are not suitable for garden cultivation. I especially admire *E. montanum*, the avalanche lily, which I have seen extending for miles up the alpine slopes of Mt. Rainier. *E. americanum* grows wild along streams at Cedaridge Farm, but its diminutive flower goes nearly unnoticed.

'Pagoda' is the best of the hybrids because it is relatively large-flowered and grows to 12 inches (30cm) high. Its nodding flower resembles a yellow Turk's cap lily and opens in spring. The leaves are lush, broad, and pointed. 'Pagoda' is best for Zones 3 to 8, and looks good partnered with snake's-head or checkered lilies (*Fritillaria meleagris*).

Plant the bulbs in autumn, 4 inches (10cm) deep, spaced 6 inches (15cm) apart in well-drained or moist soil. Although the plants prefer sun, they will thrive in light shade. It is important to provide the roots with moisture during summer dry spells.

Dogtooth violets are best planted as small colonies along woodland paths and at the edges of streams and small ponds. They are especially beautiful planted in pockets of humus-rich soil beside waterfalls in rock gardens.

Yellow flowers of dogtooth violet are similar to miniature lilies.

🌿*Eucomis comosa*

(pineapple lily)

Above: A colony of pineapple lily blooms in summer. Below: A field of freesias blankets the ground near San Diego, California.

Huge colonies of pineapple lilies grow on the slopes of the Drakensberg Mountains of South Africa. The plants produce spiky leaves and pokerlike flower stems topped by clusters of star-shaped pink, white, or green blossoms. The stem is crowned by a flower head in the shape of a pineapple, which has a tuft of leaves on top. The plants grow 2 feet (60cm) tall and flower in midsummer.

Plant the bulbs in spring, 6 inches (15cm) deep, spaced 12 inches (30cm) apart, in well-drained soil in a sunny location. Pineapple lilies are best for Zones 7 to 10, where they will successfully overwinter. In those climates where the ground freezes, the bulbs should be lifted in autumn and stored indoors.

The most effective way to display pineapple lilies is to establish a colony in mixed beds and borders and in rock gardens. They are valuable components of drought-prone landscapes, and are excellent for container plantings. Pineapple lilies also make exquisite cut flowers.

Freesia × hybrida

(florist's freesia)

Freesias are native to South Africa, where they are prolific in grassland areas. They are tender members of the iris family, growing spiky leaves and slender stems topped by trumpet-shaped flowers. Freesia flowers are highly fragrant, and grow in red, yellow, pink, orange, purple, and white, plus bicolors. There is a domestic trade in freesias as cut flowers, many of which are grown under glass, but most freesias for bulb production are grown outdoors north of San Diego in the coastal community of Gardena, where vast fields of them are visible from the highway, presenting an unexpected visual treat to passing motorists.

Plant the bulbs 5 inches (12.5cm) deep, spaced 12 inches (30cm) apart, in well-drained sandy or loam soil in full sun. Freesias are not hardy and will winter outdoors only in Zones 9 and 10, where they should be planted in autumn. In northern areas, freesias are grown as flowering potted plants in sunrooms.

Freesias make good accents in mixed perennial borders and rock gardens in frost-free areas. They are well suited to growing in containers on decks and patios, and are also good for cutting, making colorful bouquets.

Fritillaria imperialis

(crown imperial)

Crown imperials bloom at the same time as cherry and crab apple blossoms.

The genus *Fritillaria* consists of many species that make attractive landscape plants. They are recognized mostly by their nodding, bell-shaped flowers. The crown imperial is the largest-flowered of the genus, holding its cup-size blooms in pendant clusters atop 3- to 4-foot (90 to 120cm) stems. When bruised, the stems and leaves emit a musky, skunklike odor. The flower colors are yellow and orange. Other popular species include snake's-head or checkered fritillary (*F. meleagris*), which has bells patterned like a snake's skin, and Persian fritillary (*F. persica*), which has spires of maroon bells. It is said that in the mountains of Iran, where the crown imperial grows wild, new colors await discovery—especially a pink!

The bulbs of crown imperial have a depression on top that can collect water and induce rot, so drainage is especially important; *F. meleagris* will tolerate a moist soil. Plant crown imperial and Persian fritillary 5 inches (12.5cm) deep from the bottom of the bulb. They shed water best if the bulbs are planted on their sides. Snake's-head fritillary should be planted only 3 inches (7.5cm) deep. Crown imperial plants tolerate light shade, but prefer a sunny location. The plants are best for Zones 4 to 7. All varieties should be planted in autumn.

These flowers look best when planted in groups of three or more in mixed bulb borders, or as a colony at the edge of woodland. Snake's-head fritillary is good for massing along stream banks, slopes, and woodland paths.

Galanthus nivalis

(s n o w d r o p)

Snowdrops seed themselves into humus-rich soils that stay clear of weeds.

Though there are more than a hundred species of snowdrops native to Europe and Asia, they are very difficult to tell apart. All snowdrops are characterized by nodding white flowers that appear among smooth, slender green leaves in early spring, even before the last snowfalls of winter. The average plant height is just 4 to 6 inches (10 to 15cm).

Snowdrops prefer a humus-rich loam or sandy soil in sun or partial shade. Plant the pea-size bulbs in autumn 3 inches (7.5cm) deep and at least 2 inches (5cm) apart.

A harbinger of spring, snowdrops are best for edging beds and borders, where they can be easily seen. They are also attractive planted as drifts in rock gardens or colonized under deciduous trees, where leaf litter can keep the forest floor clear of weeds. They are especially beautiful combined with yellow aconites and snow crocus.

Gladiolus ×
hortulanus

(f l o r i s t ' s   g l a d i o l u s)

Florist's gladiolus is derived from crosses with wild gladiolus species native to Africa, most notably *G. byzantinus.* Beautiful spirelike plants produce sword-shaped leaves and flared blossoms, flowering in midsummer. Gladiolus has a rich flower color range that includes yellow, orange, purple, red, green, and white, plus bicolors. These plants can grow to 5 feet (1.5m) and more. Since the bulbs are sensitive to freezing, in Zones 6 and up they should be taken up in autumn after the leaves have turned brown. Over the winter, store gladiolus in a dry, dark, frost-free place.

Plant corms in the spring 5 inches (12.5cm) deep, spaced at least 6 inches (15cm) apart; wait until there is no more danger of frost. Give them full sun and a humus-rich, sandy or loam soil. Stagger plantings at two-week intervals until early summer to ensure flowers through autumn. Plants may need staking to keep them erect.

Florist's gladiolus make a good tall accent for mixed perennial borders; they combine well with daylilies and trumpet lilies.

Haemanthus katharinae

(blood lily)

Above: Gladiolus make beautiful cut flowers.
Right: Blood lilies need a frost-free environment to thrive.

The blood lily is native to South Africa, where it thrives in near-desert conditions. Although these tender bulbs will overwinter outdoors only in frost-free areas, they are valued as ornamental potted plants for early summer flowering. The plants produce bristly, globular flower heads up to 9 inches (23cm) across, composed of many spidery orange-red florets on 1- to 2-foot (30 to 60cm)-tall stems. Broad, straplike leaves surround the stems.

In mild climates, the large bulbs may be planted outdoors in autumn in a sunny position. Elsewhere, blood lilies are good for growing under glass, one to a pot. They like a well-drained sandy or loam soil, and should be planted so that the pointed neck protrudes above the soil. When growing blood lilies indoors, withhold water to establish dormancy once foliage dies down after flowering. Renew watering in autumn to repeat flowering.

These lilies are sensational planted as small colonies of nine to a dozen bulbs in frost-free areas. Otherwise, enjoy them as spectacular flowering potted plants in sunrooms and conservatories.

'Stella d' Oro' daylilies flower nonstop all summer.

Hemerocallis × hybrida
(daylily)

Most daylilies originated in China. But judging from the large numbers that grow wild along the waysides of North America, it's hard to believe they are not native wildflowers. The plants grow vigorous clumps of grasslike leaves. During the summer, long slender flower stems arise, fountainlike, from the center of the foliage. The trumpet-shaped blooms occur in an extensive color range that includes red, orange, yellow, pink, lavender blue, purple, mahogany, and bicolors. Daylilies can reach a height of 4 feet (1.2m). The dwarf daylily variety 'Stella d'Oro', developed by a Chicago daylily enthusiast, is the most prolific and the longest-flowering (from late May until autumn frost). Though daylily flowers last only a day (hence their common name), enough buds are produced on each plant to ensure a long flowering display.

Plant the tuberous roots in spring or autumn, ensuring that the roots are spread apart like an octopus, with the crown level with the soil surface. Space the tubers at least 12 inches (30cm) apart. The plants tolerate a wide range of soil conditions, though they don't do well in excessively boggy soil. Full sun or light shade suits them fine.

Daylilies are best planted as accents in mixed perennial borders. However, they make a good groundcover if planted as a colony, especially on exposed slopes that need erosion control. The dwarf varieties are suitable for containers.

Hippeastrum hybrids; amaryllis × hybrida
(amaryllis)

The versatile amaryllis can be grown in pots or beds, in full sun or light shade in frost-free and nearly frost-free areas.

The familiar Christmas amaryllis is a hybrid derived from species native to South America. Even in the wild, it has large trumpet-shaped flowers with flared, shimmering petals. Each hybrid flower can measure up to 10 inches (25cm) across, and since there can be four flowers open at once, the entire cluster can measure a spectacular 2 feet (60cm) across! Colors include mostly shades of pink, red, and orange, plus white and bicolors. Plants grow to 2 feet (60cm) tall and produce broad, arching, straplike green leaves after flowering. Sometimes as many as three flower stalks will emerge from a single bulb (the bigger the bulb the better the chance of multiple stems) over a 10-week period. In North America these amaryllis will not overwinter north of Zone 8.

Bulbs planted outdoors in Zones 8 to 10 generally take care of themselves, provided they are in full sun or light shade and have good drainage. The bulbs should be planted with the pointed end protruding above the soil and at least two thirds of the rest of the bulb in the soil, with 8-inch (20cm) spacing between them. The bulbs can be planted outdoors in autumn.

Indoor care is a bit more involved. Coaxing the bulbs to flower a second year requires keeping the leaves green and healthy after the flowers fade by regular watering and feeding with a diluted liquid house-plant fertilizer. When the danger of spring frost is past, remove the bulb from its pot and plant it in a sunny or partly shaded location outside, in fertile, humus-rich loam or sandy soil. After frost kills the leaves in autumn, dig up the bulb and brush it clean of soil. Store the bulb indoors in a frost-free, dry, dark place for several weeks. Then repot the bulb, using a sandy potting soil, and move it to a location at room temperature, with bright light.

In relatively frost-free areas, hybrid amaryllis can be grown massed in beds and cut to create spectacular exotic floral arrangements. In northern areas they are often sold prepotted as flowering house plants just requiring water. Outdoors, autumn-planted amaryllis usually bloom 4 months after planting. Some of the many exceptional varieties include 'Appleblossom' (a pink-and-white bicolor) and 'Orange Sovereign' (orange-red). Two other unusual amaryllis that produce numerous smaller flowers on shorter stems are *Hippeastrum papilli*, the striped butterfly amaryllis, and *H. gracilis* 'Scarlet Baby', a bright red. These brightly-colored flowers make wonderful gifts.

Dutch hyacinths are good companions to early tulips, such as these Kaufmanniana hybrids.

Hyacinthus orientalis
(Dutch hyacinth)

Native to the eastern Mediterranean, hyacinths are the third most popular spring-flowering bulb, ranking just below daffodils and tulips. They grow a short (about 8-inch [20cm]-tall), plump column of overlapping, fragrant, star-shaped flowers among smooth, green, pointed leaves. Their many colors include blue, red, pink, purple, apricot, yellow, and white. Hyacinths are easily forced for extra-early flowering indoors. And they are superb displayed outdoors on patios in tubs, window boxes, and barrel planters. A single flower cluster can fill an entire room with a gardenialike fragrance.

Plant bulbs in autumn, 6 inches (15cm) deep and 4 inches (10cm) apart, with the pointed side up. Hyacinths prefer full sun and a humus-rich, sandy or loam soil. The top-heavy flower heads may bend and break in the rain, necessitating a discreet support such as a short bamboo stake. After 3 years, the bulbs are best dug up and replaced with fresh stock. Hyacinths can be forced indoors in special glass containers called hyacinth vases, which allow a single bulb to be suspended over water. The roots emerge from the bulb into the water, allowing the plant to bloom indoors without soil. The best indoor flowering occurs with bulbs that have been preconditioned with 13 weeks of cold treatment. Hyacinths do best in Zones 3 to 8.

These plants are most effective when they are massed in beds and borders, or used as edging. They combine well with daffodils and Emperor tulips, especially in containers.

Hymenocallis caroliniana

(spider lily)

This native American wildflower grows in swamps from coastal Georgia south through the Gulf states and into Texas. The plants grow to 3 feet (90cm) tall, producing stiff, smooth, straplike leaves and erect flower stems. The white flowers bloom in spring with spidery filaments that extend beyond a central cup-shaped arrangement of fused petals. There are many other species of *Hymenocallis* grown in cultivation, including the fragrant, larger-flowered (and more tender) *H. narcissiflora*, also known as *Ismene calathina,* and commonly called Peruvian daffodil.

Plant the bulbs in autumn, 6 inches (15cm) deep and at least 12 inches (30cm) apart. Spider lilies prefer a moisture-retentive soil, such as a clay soil high in humus; they also tolerate boggy conditions. The Peruvian daffodil is often grown further north in old-fashioned cottage gardens, but the bulbs need to be lifted in autumn and stored indoors in a frost-free location. The spider lily prefers full sun but tolerates light shade. It performs best in Zones 8 through 10.

A wonderful early-flowering accent for streamsides and the shores of ponds, spider lily is also suitable for naturalizing in wetlands, such as damp meadows and boggy soils. The plants are salt-tolerant and are suitable for coastal gardens in mild winter areas such as the American Southeast.

A colony of spider lily thrives in its native environment—a swampy meadow near Houston, Texas.

Ipheion uniflorum

(starflower)

In sandy soil, starflower will cover the ground like stars in a galaxy.

The starflower is related to amaryllis, but is much smaller. The six-petaled, star-shaped 1-inch (2.5cm) flowers are light blue or white, and are borne in great profusion. The flowers open in the spring among clumps of grasslike leaves that remain compact, growing just 4 inches (10cm) tall. The leaves emit a strong onionlike odor when cut. Native to South America, the plant is hardy from Zones 6 through 9.

The starflower is very easy to grow in full sun or light shade, even in poor soil, if the drainage is good. Plant the marble-size bulbs in autumn, 4 inches (10cm) deep, spaced at least 3 inches (7.5cm) apart.

Starflowers will colonize any bare piece of ground or sparse grassy area through self-seeding. They are particularly attractive planted as bold drifts in rock gardens, on dry slopes, and in meadow gardens. Starflowers are also suitable for edging bulb beds and paths. Good companions include miniature daffodils, creeping phlox, species tulips, and anemones. They are featured in almost all the gardens at Colonial Williamsburg, Virginia.

Iris × *germanica*

(bearded iris)

This iris belongs to a group of complex hybrid species native to Europe. The bearded iris (also known as the German iris) grows long, strong stems topped with intricate flower heads composed of one set of broad petals that arch down (called falls) and another set that arch up (called standards). Where the petals meet is a prominent powdery cluster of stamens called a beard.

Flowering in late spring, bearded irises offer the most extensive color range of all flowering bulbs. Colors include many shades of blue, yellow, orange, pink, and red, plus white. There are even a green and a black, as well as many bicolors. The blue-green, sword-shaped leaves are arranged in a fan. Although there are many dwarf varieties no more than 12 inches (30cm) tall, the majority of bearded irises stand 3 feet (90cm) tall.

The plump, horizontal rhizomes like to bake in the sun; good growers give bearded irises beds to themselves so the rhizomes are not shaded by other plants. They should be planted with most of the rhizome beneath the soil, but with the top exposed. Although the rhizomes can be divided and transplanted from spring through fall, planting is best done in late summer. Bearded irises are heavy feeders and like a well-drained soil high in phosphorus. Some varieties are repeat-blooming in later summer or autumn if they are watered regularly during the summer. They thrive in Zones 4 south, experiencing difficulty only along the Gulf Coast, where Louisiana iris (*I. fulva*) is a better choice.

The best way to display bearded irises is to plant them as a mixture of colors. These rainbow beds can be small or large. Another good iris for displaying in gardens is *I. pseudacorus* (flag iris).

Right: A colony of blue Dutch iris looks elegant by itself. Below: Bearded iris masses on a sunny slope.

Iris hollandica
(Dutch iris)

Dutch irises are beardless irises grown commercially for florists to sell as cut flowers. They are hybrids between Spanish iris (*I. xiphium*) and two other European irises, and reproduce by bulbs rather than rhizomes. The plants grow 2 feet (60cm) tall with slender, pointed leaves. Colors include blue, yellow, bronze, purple, and white, plus bicolors; they all have yellow throats. Other good bulbous irises are *I. reticulata* (the snow iris), an extra-early flowering species in blue and purple, and also *I. sibirica*, the taller Siberian iris .

Dutch irises are not reliably hardy above Zone 8, but new bulbs planted in autumn in Zone 6 will generally overwinter and flower the first year. Plant the bulbs 5 inches (12.5cm) deep and 4 inches (10cm) apart in well-drained, sandy or loam soil in full sun. Spanish iris and snow iris are extremely hardy and will overwinter reliably into Zone 4. Siberians tolerate both dry and boggy soils.

Dutch irises are most effective when planted in groups of all one color in mixed perennial borders. They make good partners for late-flowering tulips, Siberian wallflowers, calendulas, and columbine. Snow irises are great for forming colonies in rock gardens; flag irises (*I. pseudacorus* and *I. versicolor*) are excellent for growing in poorly drained areas; bearded iris are wonderful for creating a rainbow of color in a bed all by themselves.

Above: Bronze Dutch iris flowers in company with tulips. Right: Summer snowflake adds a touch of white to woodland.

Leucojum aestivum

(summer snowflake)

Summer snowflake has bell-shaped white flowers that resemble snowdrops. Plants of *L. aestivum* grow up to 3 feet (90cm) tall, with clusters of stiff flower stems emerging from a clump of smooth, slender leaves. The best variety is 'Graveyte Giant'. This flower's common name is rather misleading since these hardy plants do not bloom in summer, but in mid- to late spring. I suppose the term "summer" is to distinguish this plant from an earlier-flowering species, *L. vernum*, which blooms in early spring. Native to Europe, summer snowflakes are suitable for Zones 4 to 8. There is also an autumn-flowering species, *L. autumnale*, which grows to 2 feet (60cm) tall, with unique stiff threadlike leaves.

Plant these bulbs in autumn, 5 inches (12.5cm) deep and at least 4 inches (10cm) apart in well-drained, humus-rich loam or sandy soil. Choose a sunny or lightly shaded position.

Summer snowflakes are good accent plants for shade gardens—particularly woodland gardens—and mixed beds. They make perfect partners for columbines, bluebells, and ostrich ferns. The flowers are excellent for cutting although the leaves must be left intact, so that they can die down to nourish the bulb so that it will bloom again the next season. The autumn-flowering species is not conspicuous in the landscape, and is more suitable for rock gardens. The delicate-looking white flowers provide a soft note among the rocks. Planting them in clumps gives them a stronger presence than they have planted individually.

Asiatic lilies in a mixture of colors grow well in the light shade of a wooded slope.

🌿 *Lilium Asiatic hybrids*
(garden lily)

Garden lilies used to have a reputation for being temperamental and difficult to grow because of disease problems, susceptibility to heat and humidity, and questionable hardiness, but the Asiatic hybrids have changed all that. Cultivars such as orange 'Enchantment' and yellow 'Connecticut King', plus the mixture called 'Mid-Century', are all as easy to grow as daffodils. Additional colors include pink, red, purple, and white. In late spring, upward-facing, chalicelike blooms grace the tops of 4-foot (1.2m)-tall strong stems surrounded by slender, lancelike leaves. Asiatic lilies are suitable for Zones 4 to 8. Another reliable lily variety is the Oriental hybrid lily 'Stargazer', with spectacular red-and-white, spotted, sideways-facing flowers.

Asiatic hybrid lilies will tolerate a wide range of soil conditions, provided the drainage is excellent. They like light shade and humus-rich soils that keep the soil cool in summer. The scaly bulbs should be planted in the spring or autumn 8 inches (20cm) deep, spaced at least 12 inches (30cm) apart. After the second season, the plants may need staking. Feed the bulbs in autumn with a high-phosphorus fertilizer. 'Stargazer' requires the same treatment as the Asiatic hybrids.

Garden lilies are good for naturalizing under a light tree canopy and at the edge of woodlands; they are also excellent planted as small colonies in mixed beds. These lilies are suitable for cutting and for containers, planted 3 bulbs to a pot.

✤*Lycoris radiata*
(spider lily)

Native to Japan, this somewhat tender plant has escaped into the wild throughout the southern United States, blooming in meadows and cemeteries, where they form beautiful colonies. Tubular florets are arranged in a spidery cluster atop erect, bare, 12-inch (30cm) stems. The most common color is scarlet, but there are also pink and yellow types. The flowers open in autumn; the leaves appear earlier in the spring. Spider lilies flourish beautifully in Zones 7 through 10.

Plant the bulbs in spring, 5 inches (12.5cm) deep, spaced 5 inches (12.5cm) apart, in well-drained, sandy or loam soil. The bulbs do best when planted in a sunny location.

Spider lilies are excellent for naturalizing where winters are mild, either as accents in mixed borders or as drifts in meadows and rock gardens. These flowers are also popular for cutting.

Spider lily grows freely in open meadows throughout the southern United States.

✤*Lycoris squamigera*
(naked lady, magic lily)

Native to Japan, this hardy plant is suitable for growing outdoors in Zones 4 to 8. It first produces a clump of slender, smooth, arching leaves in the spring, which die down by early summer. Next, naked, 3-foot (90cm)-tall flower stems rise from the middle of the plant, topped with clusters of up to eight pink trumpet-shaped blooms. The flowers resemble those of a tender bulb suitable for Zones 8 to 10, *Amaryllis belladonna*, which is also known as naked lady.

For many years I wondered how this flowering bulb received the common name magic lily, until I moved a colony. In spite of digging up and transplanting what I thought was every bulb to the other end of the garden, the next season I discovered *twice* as many flowering plants in the original location—like magic.

Plant the bulbs in spring, 6 inches (15cm) deep and at least 6 inches (15cm) apart. They demand full sun, and well-drained, fertile, sandy or loam soil.

These plants are best when massed to form colonies in meadows, on sunny banks, and in mixed borders, where they will keep blooming for years, living up to their common name.

Left: Blue grape hyacinths flow like a river at Keukenhof Gardens. Above: Colonies of naked ladies, such as this one, are suitable for planting between dwarf shrubs and as accents in rock gardens.

Muscari armeniacum
(grape hyacinth)

Although there is a species of grape hyacinth native to the eastern woodlands and meadows of North America, the grape hyacinth commonly grown in gardens comes from Armenia. Intense blue, bell-shaped florets are clustered on a cone-shaped flower spike among smooth, slender leaves. Flowering occurs in early spring. This plant is suitable for Zones 4 to 8.

Plant bulbs 4 inches (10cm) deep, at least 2 inches (5cm) apart, in autumn. Grape hyacinths prefer full sun, though they tolerate light shade and demand good drainage.

They are good for edging beds and borders and are also pretty planted as drifts in rock gardens. At Keukenhof Gardens in Holland, grape hyacinths are massed under trees to create a unique river of blue.

A bed of giant trumpet-flowered daffodil 'Fortissimo' blooms among celandine ground cover.

Narcissus ✕ hybrida
(daffodils)

The Pyrenees, the mountain range of northern Spain, is home to more species of daffodils than any other region, but the best daffodil varieties today are bred mainly by the British, followed by the Dutch. The main parents of modern daffodils are *Narcissus poeticus* and *N. pseudonarcissus*. There are twelve classifications, varying in size from the giant trumpet daffodils to the little cyclamen hybrids (see pages 81–82). Most are fragrant, and they are characterized by an outer rim of swept-back petals and a protruding trumpet, or cup. Although the dominant color is yellow, there are white varieties and bicolors. In some varieties, the cup can be orange or pink. At Cedaridge Farm, my favorite varieties are 'Professor Einstein', for its porcelain white outer petals and huge, flat, deep orange cup; the yellow-and-orange bicolor 'Fortissimo', for its huge size; and 'Pink Charm', for its impressive pink-and-yellow cup.

Plant the bulbs in autumn, 8 inches (20cm) deep for the large-flowered types and 6 inches (15cm) deep for the smaller kinds. Space plants at least 4 inches (10cm) apart, in humus-rich, well-drained soil in full sun. Although daffodils will tolerate light shade, they have a tendency to diminish in vigor when planted in deep shade.

Daffodils are the easiest of all bulbs to naturalize if the slender leaves are left to die down by themselves. The large-flowered daffodils are best for naturalizing at the edges of woodland or lawn because they stand out in the landscape and the dying foliage doesn't look unsightly. Miniatures are best for rock gardens and containers. Even the miniatures have long stems, so nearly all daffodil varieties are excellent for cutting gardens, mixed borders, and along paths.

Star of Bethlehem will quickly colonize open fields, flowering in spring.

Ornithogalum umbellatum

(star-of-Bethlehem)

There are many species of *Ornithogalum*, most of which resemble wild onions (*Allium*). Many are native to North and South Africa, and they are too tender for northern gardens. The hardiest by far is *O. umbellatum*. Although native to the Mediterranean, it has adapted so well to North America that it has escaped into the wild and seeded itself into open meadows and along waysides. The plants, which are hardy in Zones 4 to 8, grow clumps of grasslike leaves, and in the spring they are covered with pure white star-shaped flowers. The hardy *O. nutans* is similar in appearance, but its green-tinted star-shaped flowers are arranged on an upright spike. It flowers earlier, and prefers Zones 6 to 8. *O. thyrsoides* features spiky flower clusters, and it is hardy in Zones 8 south. It is often grown as a flowering potted plant further north.

Plant the pea-size bulbs in autumn, 2 inches (5cm) deep and at least 2 inches (5cm) apart, in well-drained soil in a sunny location.

Star-of-Bethlehem is good for edging beds, massing to create colonies in rock gardens, and naturalizing in meadow gardens. It is especially lovely in the company of bluebells and is suitable for window boxes.

Polianthes tuberosa

(tuberose)

Native to Mexico, tuberoses are one of the most sweetly fragrant flowering bulbs you can grow, with an aroma reminiscent of gardenias. The plants grow poker-straight stems, with slender, pointed leaves, to 3 feet (90cm) tall. In late summer, clusters of tubular white flowers appear. In some varieties the flowers are double, but the single variety has the strongest scent. Just one stem in a vase can fill an entire room with fragrance. Although the plants are hardy from Zone 7 south, they rarely make satisfactory flower stalks after the first season. It is always best to start with new bulb stock each spring, planted after the danger of frost is past.

Spires of tuberose grow through stems of dahlia at Cedaridge Farm.

Plant the rhizomes in the spring, 3 inches (7.5cm) deep in fertile, humus-rich, sandy or loam soil in full sun. Space bulbs at least 6 inches (15cm) apart. Tuberoses should usually be planted in sheltered positions since the tall, slender stems easily topple over.

Tuberoses are highly valued as cut flowers, and are often seen planted in long straight rows as components of cutting gardens. They are also valued for mixing with other white flowers such as moonflowers, gladiolus, and phlox in all-white gardens, moonlight gardens, and fragrance gardens. Try planting them close to the front door so visitors to your home can enjoy their very pleasant aroma. Tuberoses are perfect partners for gladiolus and dahlias in old-fashioned cottage gardens. They flower from the bottom up; pick them when the lowest flowers start to open, and the remaining flowers will open to make a long-lasting cut-flower display.

Persian buttercups grow in sunny areas, like this production field near San Diego, California.

Ranunculus asiaticus
(Persian buttercup)

Related to buttercups and native to the eastern Mediterranean, this tender spring-flowering bulb has blossoms that resemble poppies, with silky, iridescent petals and a central crown of powdery black stamens. With flowers available in red, yellow, orange, pink, apricot, and white, the plants grow to 18 inches (45cm) tall and have fernlike foliage. Modern varieties are mostly hybrids, with many layers of petals forming a globe effect. Although these buttercups overwinter reliably only in Zones 8 through 10, when left in the garden, they merely require frost protection. At Cedaridge Farm, we grow a crop of 'Tecalote Hybrids' in special cold frames sheltered from the wind.

Plant bulbs in autumn, 5 inches (12.5cm) deep, spaced 4 inches (10cm) apart. They demand a sunny position and well-drained sandy soil as well as protection from frost. They are so beautiful that it's worth growing them in pots in northern gardens, along with some De Caen anemones, which bloom simultaneously and require similar treatment.

In frost-free areas, Persian buttercups are good for massed bedding displays in a mixture of colors. They are also spectacular planted in containers and grouped among Dutch irises and anemones in mixed borders. In the North they are popular as flowering indoor potted plants grown under glass.

Scilla campanulata
(Spanish bluebells)

These hardy spring-flowering bulbs resemble English bluebells, but they are much more widely adapted—and showier—than the true English bluebell. Spanish bluebells are native to northern Spain. They are also listed botanically as *Endymion hispanicus*, *Scilla hispanica*, and *Hyacinthoides hispanica*. Plants grow to 10 inches (25cm) tall and produce strong arching stems clustered along their length with pendant bell-shaped flowers. The leaves are slender, smooth, and dark green. Although the English bluebell is fragrant, Spanish bluebells are not. Flower colors include blue, pink, and white.

Plant the bulbs in autumn, 4 inches (10cm) deep and 4 inches (10cm) apart in full sun or light shade. The soil should be well-drained and high in humus content. These plants grow best in Zones 4 to 8.

Spanish bluebells are invaluable for naturalizing along woodland paths and on sunny slopes. They are also good for grouping among mixed perennials such as primroses and bleeding hearts, and between shrubs such as azaleas, which bloom at the same time.

A colony of Spanish bluebells makes a purple-hued tableau in company with azaleas, hostas, and an ostrich fern at Cedaridge Farm.

Naturalized Peruvian squill flourishes on a sunny slope in a coastal California garden.

Scilla peruviana

(Peruvian squill)

You would think from its botanical and common names that this plant is from Peru. Wrong! It's from North Africa, where it grows in profusion along the waysides on the road to Marrakesh. It flowers in the spring with impressive dome-shaped flower clusters composed of star-shaped, deep blue florets, held erect above rosettes of succulent, strappy leaves. A somewhat tender plant, Peruvian squill is best for Zones 8 through 10. In other locations, this plant does well in pots.

Plant the bulbs in autumn, 5 inches (12.5cm) deep, spaced 6 inches (15cm) apart. Choose a sunny location with well-drained sandy or loam soil.

Peruvian squill is best planted in colonies to naturalize on sunny slopes and in rock gardens. It is a good choice to force for early flowering as a potted plant and its flowers are suitable for cutting.

Above: Nodding blue flowers of Siberian squill bloom in the sun. Below: A bed of harlequin flower displays its mixture of colors.

Scilla sibirica
(S i b e r i a n   s q u i l l)

In the wilds of the Caucasus Mountains of Russia, where they are native, Siberian squills grow so thickly among patches of melting snow that they resemble pools of water. The nodding, star-shaped blue flowers appear in early spring among clusters of slender, crocuslike leaves.

Plant the bulbs in autumn, 4 inches (10cm) deep and 4 inches apart in well-drained, humus-rich soil in sun or light shade. This plant self-sows prolifically and grows best in Zones 3 to 8.

Siberian squill is one of the hardiest of all flowering bulbs, but is greatly underused in northern bulb gardens. It is an ideal plant to edge daffodil beds, where the combination creates a magnificent yellow and blue harmony. It also naturalizes on sunny slopes and in light shade under deciduous trees.

Sparaxis tricolor
(h a r l e q u i n   f l o w e r)

The harlequin flower is similar in appearance to baboon flower, freesia, and corn lily (to which it is closely related). These South African wildflowers are not hardy, and will overwinter reliably only in Zones 8 south or under the protection of glass. The 8-inch(20cm)-tall plants produce beautiful star-shaped flowers in a magnificent color range that includes red, pink, orange, and white, with a black or maroon zone surrounding a bright yellow eye. The spiky leaves resemble iris foliage. 'Tecalote Hybrids' are a particularly good American-bred mixture, with extra-large flowers.

Plant the bulbs in autumn, 5 inches (12.5cm) deep, spaced 4 inches (10cm) apart. They require full sun and prefer well-drained sandy soil. In northern gardens, harlequin flowers will bloom from a spring planting after danger of hard freezes has passed.

Sparaxis is good for massing in rock gardens and along sunny paths. Harlequin flowers look sensational in containers, and they are valued for cutting. Bulbs can remain in the same pot for years, until there are too many of them.

Summer crocus is much underused in most home gardens. Plant it in generous colonies.

❧ *Sternbergia lutea*

(winter daffodil, summer crocus)

Huge colonies of these tender bulbs grow by the wayside in southern Italy and Greece. The common name winter daffodil is a misnomer since the flowers neither resemble daffodils nor bloom in winter. The goblet-shaped, cruciuslike yellow flowers are produced in late summer or early autumn on bare 5-inch (12.5cm)-tall stems, after the slender, arching leaves have died down. Winter daffodils are best for Zones 6 through 9. The variety 'Major' has the largest flowers.

Plant the bulbs in summer, 5 inches (12.5cm) deep, spaced at least 4 inches (10cm) apart. The soil should be well-drained in full sun.

The winter daffodil is invaluable for late summer color, especially when it is planted as an edging for mixed borders. The yellow of these blooms makes a beautiful partner to the blue mist shrub (*Caryopteris incana*) and also a good companion for pink and blue autumn-flowering crocus.

✿ *Tigridia pavonia*
(t i g e r   f l o w e r)

This relative of the iris comes from Mexico, where it grows profusely along coastal stream banks. It has curious three-petaled flowers in a wonderful array of colors that includes yellow, red, pink, and white. The flowers, beautifully enhanced with conspicuous spots, can measure up to 4 inches (10cm) across. The irislike, green leaves are ribbed and shaped like swords.

Tiger flower is related to iris, but, unlike some iris species, will survive winters only in frost-free areas.

Tiger flowers can be grown from seed to flower the first year, but growing them from bulbs is more reliable. They are summer-flowering, grow 3 feet (90cm) tall, and will overwinter in frost-free areas. The tiger flower performs best in Zones 7 through 10.

Plant the corms in the spring, 3 inches (7.5cm) deep, spaced at least 6 inches (15cm) apart. They prefer a sunny position and a sandy or loam soil with good drainage. Where the ground freezes in winter, lift the bulbs in autumn and store them in a frost-free location for replanting in the spring. For flowering in late summer, start seeds indoors at least 8 weeks before outdoor planting.

Tiger flowers make good accents for mixed borders. They are particularly desirable as a pond or streamside plant. Although each flower lasts only a day, plants produce so many buds that flowering extends for several weeks. The flower petals have a shimmering, satiny look that makes them stand out in a crowd; this is a plant that deserves to be much more widely grown.

Tulipa × hybrida
(tulip)

Most modern varieties of tulips are descended from a wild species, *Tulipa gesnerana*, which is native to Turkey. The classic tulip has an urn-shaped bloom on a long, strong stem up to 18 inches (45cm) high, but the flower form can vary from the large-flowered feathered parrot tulips to the large, double peony-flowered kinds. The color range is extensive, including red, orange, yellow, purple, pink, maroon, green, and white, plus bicolors. The only important color missing is a sky blue. Tulip leaves are usually broad, spear-shaped, and pointed.

Culture depends on variety, although all tulip bulbs should be planted in autumn. The modern hybrids are best planted 5 inches (12.5cm) deep and 4 inches (10cm) apart in a sunny or lightly shaded location with good drainage. When cutting, leave at least two leaves to help the bulb regenerate for another season of bloom. However, after a second season the quality of modern hybrids usually diminishes and the bulbs need replanting. The original wild species tulips, as well as a group known as the botanicals, are much more successful at naturalizing and coming back every year. These include Kaufmanniana hybrids, the Fosteriana hybrids, the Greigii hybrids, and easy-to-grow wildlings like *T. tarda* and *T. turkistanica*.

Modern hybrid tulips are best used for massing in beds and borders, as pretty accents in mixed perennial borders, and for cutting. Most botanicals and species tulips are better grown as drifts in rock gardens and as edgings for beds and borders. Some of the best varieties for forcing and growing in containers include 'Apricot Beauty', 'Kees Nelis', and 'Merry Widow'. When buying tulips you will find them described as early- (late April), midseason- (early May), and late- (mid-May) flowering.

These double-flowered and single-flowered tulips group around the trunk of a crab apple.

Watsonia beatricis

(b u g l e   l i l y)

Bugle lily grows among lily of the Nile in Kirstenbosch Garden, Cape Town, South Africa.

In spring throughout South Africa, the bugle lily is the dominant wildflower in open fields and meadows, growing beautiful, erect, pokerlike flower stems studded with mostly orange flowers, up to 4 feet (1.2m) high. The spiky leaves are bright green and resemble irises. The color range is more extensive with a taller species, *W. pyramidata* (including red, pink, and white). But since it grows 6 feet (1.8m) tall, it tends to be a little too large for most home garden situations.

Both these plants are tender except in Zones 8 south. In spite of this, several bulb specialists offer bugle lilies as annuals, to be lifted after frost and stored indoors over the winter. Plant the bulbs 6 inches (15cm) deep and 6 inches (15cm) apart. The soil should be reasonably well-drained and in a sunny location. These plants are suitable for growing in containers.

Bugle lily is beautiful massed on sunny slopes and combines well with blue agapanthus. It is an excellent component of drought-tolerant gardens and rock gardens and is good for cutting.

Worsleya rayneri
(blue amaryllis)

Mature flowering-size blue amaryllis bulbs are so scarce that they are rarely offered by bulb specialists, although seed is sometimes available. Unfortunately, flowering from seed can take up to 7 years. The flowers of the blue amaryllis are the size of regular amaryllis, and they are a true blue. A word of caution: it is vital that you buy seeds and bulbs only from a reputable supplier. A friend paid twenty dollars for three seeds of a very rare blue amaryllis and waited patiently for seven years until the plant bloomed. It produced only common red flowers!

The baseball-size bulbs have long, pointed necks. They should be planted in autumn so the necks protrude through the soil surface. Although the plants are tender and must be kept in bright light above 55°F (13°C), they can be grown in pots indoors. Give them full sun and good drainage.

In Zones 9 and 10, it is worth trying to establish a colony of these spectacular flowering bulbs on a sunny slope or in a rock garden. Elsewhere, blue amaryllis must be grown as a potted plant, blooming in late summer.

The blue amaryllis is probably the most treasured flowering bulb you can grow.

✽❧*Zantedeschia aethiopica*
(c a l l a   l i l y)

Calla lilies grow wild along stream banks and marshes throughout Africa. They have also naturalized on marshy soil along the California coast. Botanically speaking, they are not lilies, but arums. Like their arum relatives, they grow lustrous dark green leaves and erect stems topped by white flowers consisting of a hooded spadix and powdery yellow stamens. The plants grow 3 feet (90cm) tall. There is also a taller variety called 'Green Goddess'. Calla lilies are mostly spring-flowering.

Calla 'Green Goddess' has green-tipped flower spathes and wavy, dark green leaves.

Although calla lilies are tender and grow best in Zones 7 to 10, they can be grown in pots and then moved indoors to keep them alive during the winter in colder areas. Plant the bulbs in spring, 6 inches (15cm) deep in moist, boggy, or humus-rich loam soil in sun or light shade. Space plants at least 12 inches (30cm) apart.

Callas are good for growing along the shores of streams and ponds, or as accents in mixed perennial borders. There are several species and hybrids of calla that extend the color range to pink, yellow, and red. These are not as large-flowered as *Z. aethiopica*, and less than half the height, but they are especially valued for cutting.

These white flowers can be an original element of mixed flower bouquets, or just one or two calla lilies can be carried by bridesmaids in a wedding processional as unique and striking accessories.

Zephyranthes atamasco

(atamasco lily)

Native to the southeastern United States, this relative of the amaryllis has trumpet-shaped flowers that are mostly white, and slender, grasslike, arching green leaves. Plants grow just 8 inches (20cm) tall, flower in spring, and overwinter in Zones 7 through 10. There are several more tender species, suitable for Zones 9 and 10. The best is a pink-flowered species, *Z. grandiflora* (rain lily), which has the ability to flower all summer after heavy rains but remains dormant during droughts.

Plant the bulbs in autumn, 5 inches (12.5cm) deep, 4 inches (10cm) apart, in well-drained sandy or loam soil. Choose a location in full sun or light shade.

These lilies are easily naturalized since they seed themselves into sandy soil. They are good for planting along lightly shaded paths, especially among southern azaleas and on sunny slopes, and combine well with camellias and azaleas. They are prolific in cemeteries throughout the South, where antique flower varieties thrive, not having been disturbed for decades.

Atamasco lilies thrive in their native habitat —a cypress swamp near Charleston, South Carolina.

About
the
Author

Derek Fell is a writer and photographer who specializes in gardening, with an emphasis on step-by-step gardening concepts and garden design. He lives in Bucks County, Pennsylvania, at historic Cedaridge Farm, Tinicum Township, where he cultivates extensive award-winning flower and vegetable gardens that have been featured in *Architectural Digest, Garden Design, Beautiful Gardens, Gardens Illustrated, American Nurseryman,* and *Mid-Atlantic Country* magazines. Born and educated in England, he first worked for seven years with Europe's largest seed company, then moved to Pennsylvania in 1964 to work for Burpee Seeds as their catalog manager, a position he held for six years before taking on duties as executive director of the All-America Selections (the national seed trials) and the National Garden Bureau (an information office sponsored by the American seed industry). Now the author of more than fifty garden books and calendars, he has traveled widely throughout North America, also documenting gardens in Europe, Africa, New Zealand, and Asia. His most recent books are *Renoir's Garden* (Simon & Schuster), *The Impressionist Garden* (Crown), *500 Perennial Garden Ideas* (Simon & Schuster), and *The Pennsylvania Gardener* (Camino Books).

A frequent contributor to *Architectural Digest* and *Woman's Day* magazines, Derek Fell is the winner of more awards from the Garden Writers Association of America than any other garden writer. He also worked as a consultant on gardening to the White House during the Ford Administration.

Wall calendars, greeting cards, and art posters featuring Derek Fell's photography are published worldwide. He has lectured on photography and the gardens of the great Impressionist painters at numerous art museums, including the Smithsonian Institution in Washington, D.C.; the Philadelphia Museum of Art and the Barnes Foundation, Philadelphia; and the Denver Art Museum, Colorado. He is also host of a regular garden show for the QVC cable television shopping channel, entitled *Step-by-Step Gardening,* which is plugged into fifty million homes.

Fell's highly acclaimed *Step-by-Step Gardening* mail-order perennial plant catalogs for Spring Hill Nurseries (North America's largest mail-order nursery) reach an audience of home gardeners estimated to be more than three million in spring and autumn. He is a former president of the Hobby Greenhouse Association, a former director of the Garden Writers Association of America, the president of the International Test Gardeners Association, and a cofounder of the American Gardening Association.

A complete list of published works follows.

Books by Derek Fell

(An asterisk indicates coauthorship.)

The White House Vegetable Garden. 1976, Exposition.

House Plants for Fun & Profit. 1978, Bookworm.

How to Photograph Flowers, Plants, & Landscapes. 1980, HP Books.

Vegetables: How to Select, Grow, and Enjoy. 1982, HP Books.

Annuals: How to Select, Grow, and Enjoy. 1983, HP Books.

Deerfield: An American Garden Through Four Seasons. 1986, Pidcock Press.

Trees & Shrubs. 1986, HP Books.

Garden Accents. 1987, Henry Holt. (*Inspired Garden* in the United Kingdom)

Discover Anguilla. 1988, Caribbean Concepts.

Home Landscaping. 1988, Simon & Schuster.

The One-Minute Gardener. 1988, Running Press.

A Kid's First Gardening Book. 1989, Running Press.

Three Year Garden Journal. 1989, Starwood.

Ornamental Grass Gardening. 1989, HP Books.

The Complete Garden Planning Manual. 1989, HP Books.

The Essential Gardener. 1990, Crown.

Essential Roses. 1990, Crown.

Essential Annuals. 1990, Crown.

Essential Bulbs. 1990, Crown.

Essential Herbs. 1990, Crown.

Essential Perennials. 1990, Crown.

Essential Shrubs. 1990, Crown.

The Easiest Flower to Grow. 1990, Ortho.

550 Home Landscaping Ideas. 1991, Simon & Schuster.

Renoir's Garden. 1991, Simon & Schuster.

Beautiful Bucks County. 1991, Cedaridge.

The Encyclopedia of Ornamental Grasses. 1992, Smithmark.

The Encyclopedia of Flowers. 1993, Smithmark.

Garden Guide: Annuals. 1993, Smithmark.

Garden Guide: Perennials. 1993, Smithmark.

Garden Guide: Bulbs. 1993, Smithmark.

Garden Guide: Roses. 1993, Smithmark.

550 Perennial Garden Ideas. 1993, Simon & Schuster.

The Impressionist Garden. 1994, Crown.

Practical Gardening. 1995, Friedman/Fairfax.

Gardens of Philadelphia & the Delaware Valley. 1995, Temple University Press.

The Pennsylvania Gardener. 1995, Camino Books.

In the Garden with Derek. 1995, Camino Books.

Glorious Flowers. 1996, Friedman/Fairfax.

Perennial Gardening with Derek Fell. 1996, Friedman/Fairfax.

Vegetable Gardening with Derek Fell. 1996, Friedman/Fairfax

Calendars

For Your Gardens (Portal)

Great Gardens (Portal)

Monet's Garden (Portal)

The Impressionist Garden (Portal)

The Gardening Year (Portal)

Perennials (Starwood)

Flowering Shrubs (Starwood)

Flowering Bulbs (Starwood)

Northeast Gardens Calendar (Starwood)

Mid-Atlantic Gardens Calendar (Starwood)

Southern Gardens Calendar (Starwood)

California Gardens Calendar (Starwood)

Pacific Northwest Gardens Calendar (Starwood)

Art Posters

Deerfield Garden (Portal)

Spring Garden (Portal)

Monet's Bridge (Portal)

Monet's Roses (Palm Press)

Monet's Scarlet Climber (Palm Press)

Sources

The following mail-order suppliers specialize in flowering bulbs.

Spring- and Summer- Flowering Bulbs

Bakker of Holland
Box 50
Louisiana, MO 63353

Brecks
Box 1757
Peoria, IL 61656

Burpee Bulbs
300 Park Avenue
Warminster, PA 18974

Dutch Gardens
Box 200
Adelphia, NJ 07710

Earl May Nursery Co.
Box 500
Shenandoah, IA 51603

International Growers
   Exchange
Box 52248
Livonia, MI 48152

J.W. Jung Co.
335 S. High Street
Randolph, WI 53957

Messelaar Bulb Co.
Box 269
Ipswich, MA 01938

Charles H. Mueller
River Road
New Hope, PA 18938

Park Seed Co.
Box 46
Greenwood, SC 29648

Peter De Jager Bulb Co.
Box 2010
South Hamilton, MA
   01982

Pinetree Garden Seeds
Route 100N
Gloucester, ME 04260

John Scheepers, Inc.
63 Wall Street
New York, NY 10005

Ty Ty Plantation
Box 159
Ty Ty, GA 31795

Van Engelen, Inc.
307 Maple Street
Litchfield, CT 06759

Wayside Gardens
Box 1
Hodges, SC 29695

White Flower Farm
Route 63
Litchfield, CT 06759

Amaryllis

Amaryllis, Inc.
Box 318
Baton Rouge, LA 78021

Dahlias

Legg Dahlia Gardens
1069 Hastings Road
Geneva, NY 14456

Swan Island Dahlias
Box 800
Canby, OR 97013

Daylilies

Daylily Discounters
1 Daylily Plaza
Alachua, FL 32615

Snow Creek Daylily
   Gardens
Box 2007
Port Townsend, WA
   98368

Gladiolus

Gladside Gardens
61 Main Street
Northfield, MA 01360

Heirloom Bulbs

Old House Gardens
536 Third Street
Ann Arbor, MI 48103

Irises

Cooley's Gardens
Box 126
Silverton, OR 97381

Schreiner's Gardens
3625 Quinaby Road NE
Salem, OR 97303

Lilies

B & D Lilies
Box 2007
Port Townsend, WA
   98368

Rex Bulb Farms
Box 774
Port Townsend, WA
   98368

Narcissus

The Daffodil Mart
Box 794
Gloucester, MA 23061

Grant Mitsch Novelty
  Daffodils
Box 218
Hubbard, OR 97032

Tulips

Veldheer Tulip Gardens
12755 Quincy Street
Holland, MI 49424

Canada

C.A. Cruikshank, Inc.
1015 Mount Pleasant Road
Toronto, Ontario
M4P 2M1

Gardenimport, Inc.
Box 760
Thornhill, Ontario
L3T 4A5

THE USDA PLANT HARDINESS MAP
OF NORTH AMERICA

RANGE OF AVERAGE
ANNUAL MINIMUM
TEMPERATURES FOR
EACH ZONE

ZONE 1   BELOW -50° F
ZONE 2   -50° TO -40°
ZONE 3   -40° TO -30°
ZONE 4   -30° TO -20°
ZONE 5   -20° TO -10°
ZONE 6   -10° TO   0°
ZONE 7   0° TO 10°
ZONE 8   10° TO 20°
ZONE 9   20° TO 30°
ZONE 10 30° TO 40°
ZONE 11 ABOVE 40°

Index